ASSASSINATION!

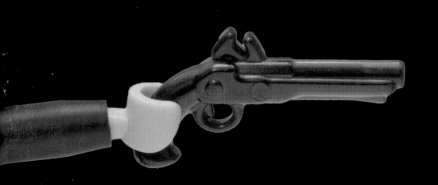

BRENDAN POWELL SMITH

ASSASSINATION!

THE BRICK CHRONICLE OF ATTEMPTS ON THE LIVES OF TWELVE US PRESIDENTS

268676

Skyhorse Publishing, Inc.
New York

Skyhorse Publishing books may be purchased in bulk at special discounts for sales promotion, corporate gifts, fund-raising, or educational purposes. Special editions can also be created to specifications. For details, contact the Special Sales Department, Skyhorse Publishing, 307 West 36th Street, 11th Floor, New York, NY 10018 or info@skyhorsepublishing.com.

Skyhorse® and Skyhorse Publishing® are registered trademarks of Skyhorse Publishing, Inc.®, a Delaware corporation.

Visit our website at www.skyhorsepublishing.com.

10 9 8 7 6 5 4 3 2 1

Library of Congress Cataloging-in-Publication Data

Smith, Brendan Powell.
 Assassination! : the brick chronicle presents attempts on the lives of twelve US presidents / Brendan Powell Smith.
     pages cm
 Includes bibliographical references.
 ISBN 978-1-62087-998-6 (hardcover : alk. paper) 1. Presidents--Assassination--United States--History--Juvenile literature.
 2. Presidents--Assassination attempts--United States--History--Juvenile literature. 3. LEGO toys--Juvenile literature. I. Title.
 E176.1.S644 2013
 364.152'40973--dc23
                               2013018382

Printed in China

Editor: Julie Matysik
Designer: Brian Peterson
Managing Editor: Abigail Gehring

For Lucia, Jessica, and Lila.

"Assassination is not an American practice or habit, and one so vicious and so desperate cannot be engrafted into our political system. This conviction of mine has steadily gained strength since the Civil War began. Every day's experience confirms it."

—William Seward, 1862

Chapter 1
ANDREW JACKSON
January 30, 1835

A cold, damp January morning in 1835: Andrew Jackson exits the Capitol building where he has just attended a funeral service for a congressman.

Leaning on his cane and on Treasury Secretary Levi Woodbury for support, the sixty-seven-year-old president approaches the Capitol steps, unaware of the lurking danger just behind the next pillar.

Suddenly, a flamboyantly dressed man emerges in front of the president with a pistol aimed directly at Jackson's chest. Standing only six feet away from his target, he pulls the trigger and a loud bang is heard.

Another loud bang, but the second pistol also misfires.
By this time, Jackson has become outraged and charges
at the assassin with his cane.

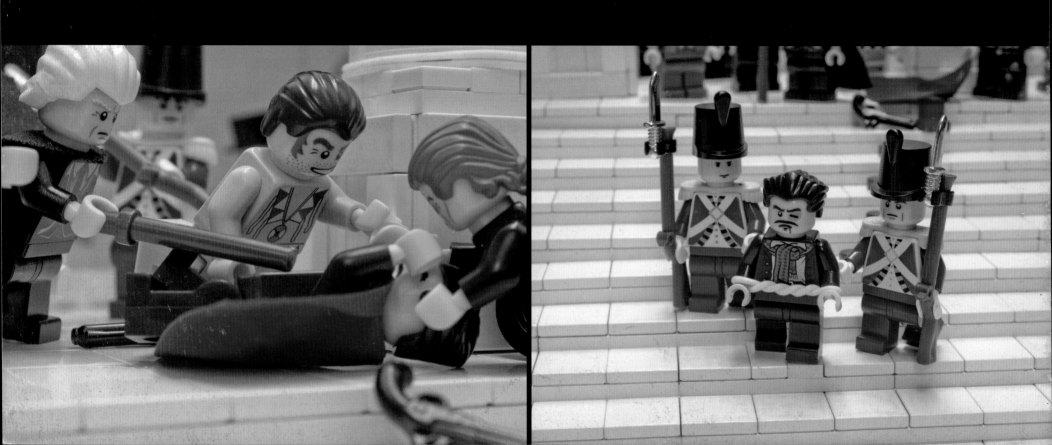

Born in England, Lawrence came to the United States with his family at age twelve, and settled in Washington, DC. He was described as a mild-mannered, well-behaved boy.

He worked as a house painter until his early thirties, when those who knew him say his personality underwent a radical transformation.

Quitting his job, Lawrence grew a mustache and began purchasing extravagant outfits that he would silently model in his doorway for passersby, sometimes changing outfits three or four times a day.

He would also rent pairs of horses and hire a prostitute to accompany him on regal processions through the streets of Washington.

Believing himself to be King Richard III of England, he explained to his bewildered sister and her husband that there was no longer any need for him to work, as the US government owed him a vast sum of money.

Lawrence saw President Jackson's opposition to the establishment of a national bank as holding up this payment. In the weeks before his attack, Lawrence was overheard talking to himself in his paint shop, saying, "Damn him, he does not know his enemy; I will put a pistol . . . Erect a gallows . . . Damn General Jackson! Who's General Jackson?"

At his trial, Lawrence was prone to wild rants and refused to recognize the legitimacy of the proceedings, at one point saying solemnly to the courtroom, "It is for me, gentlemen, to pass upon you, and not you upon me."

In the end, the judge, jury, and even his prosecutor, famed composer of "The Star-Spangled Banner," Francis Scott Key, were convinced that Lawrence could not be held criminally responsible for his crime.

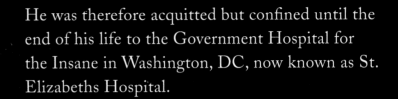

He was therefore acquitted but confined until the end of his life to the Government Hospital for the Insane in Washington, DC, now known as St. Elizabeths Hospital.

Later testing of the pistols used by Lawrence in the attack found them to be in perfect working order, firing successfully and accurately. It has been said that the odds of both pistols misfiring is 125,000 to 1. It is likely the damp weather contributed to their failure.

President Jackson was seemingly unperturbed by the attempt on his life and had become accustomed to receiving death threats by mail. One such letter read: "You dam'd old Scoundrel . . . I will cut your throat whilst you are sleeping. I wrote to you repeated Cautions, so look out or damn you I'll have you burnt at the Stake."

It was signed by the acclaimed Shakespearean actor, Junius Brutus Booth, with the postscript: "You know me! Look out!" Though it was dismissed as a forgery at the time, 175 years later, scholars verified that the letter was indeed penned by the father of John Wilkes Booth.

Chapter 2

ABRAHAM LINCOLN
August 1864

After three years of civil war and hundreds of thousands of casualties on both sides, the Union was finally gaining a clear advantage over an increasingly desperate Confederacy.

The president rode the rest of the way at a fast pace, working hard to regain control of his horse, and eventually arriving by the guarded gate.

Retracing Lincoln's route, the guard later found Lincoln's hat, and, on inspection, discovered a bullet hole through it.

When the hat was returned to him, Lincoln asked that the matter not be made public, and added that, "I long ago made up my mind that if anybody wants to kill me, he will do it . . . It seems to me, the man who would succeed me would be just as objectionable to my enemies—if I have any."

Chapter 3

ABRAHAM LINCOLN
April 14, 1865

Son to the most famous Shakespearean actor of his day, young John Wilkes Booth carried on his family's tradition. Three years into his acting career, at age twenty, he was proclaimed the handsomest actor on the American stage.

By 1861, at age twenty-three, Booth was starring in lead roles in theaters in New York, Boston, Chicago, and St. Louis, earning $20,000 a year (equivalent to about $500,000 today), and reviewers considered him the most promising young actor in America.

Young women from the North and the South found Booth's refined charms and dashing good looks irresistible, and he never had trouble finding female companionship.

Booth did not enlist as a soldier, but chose to use his personal wealth and special privilege as an actor to move freely about the country as a way to smuggle badly needed medical supplies to the South.

At the same time, Booth also courted Lucy Hale, the daughter of an abolitionist US senator from New Hampshire, and they became secretly engaged to marry.

By the time of Lincoln's reelection in late 1864, the war was going increasingly poorly for the South. Booth turned his attentions away from acting and began recruiting a band of loyal friends to assist in a decisive action he desperately hoped might turn the tide of the war.

The plan was to abduct President Lincoln from a theater, knocking him unconscious as the lights were turned out, then spirit away their captive to Virginia, where Lincoln would be held as ransom for the release of thousands of Confederate prisoners of war.

But upon peering inside, they discovered the president was not on board. Lincoln had changed his plans and was at that moment attending a function at the very hotel in Washington where Booth was staying.

Worrying that their botched plan would arouse suspicion, the group fled. After this incident, two of Booth's conspirators decided they would no longer participate in Booth's plans.

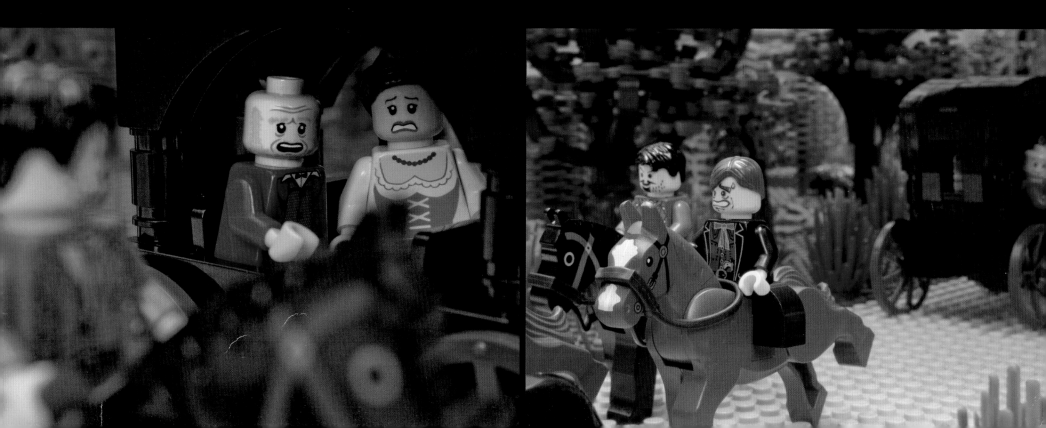

The next few weeks saw the fall of the Confederate capital at Richmond and the surrender of the commander of the Confederate Army, General Robert E. Lee, at the Appomattox Court House in Virginia. The defeat of the South was certain.

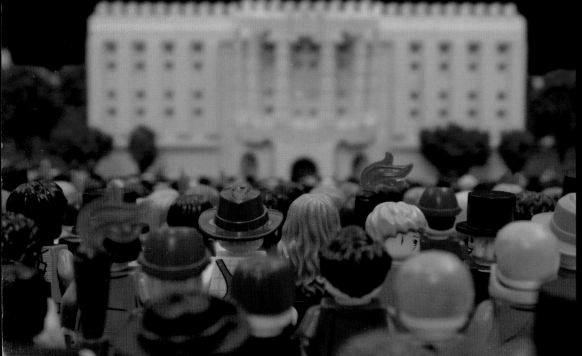

In Washington the mood became jubilant. On the night of April 11, a crowd of thousands of celebrants converged upon the White House to hear the president make an address.

Lincoln emerged on a small balcony, and lit by a lantern held by his son, Tad, he spoke about the future, and for the first time publicly spoke about the right to vote for freed male slaves: "I would myself prefer that it were now conferred on the very intelligent, and those who served our cause as soldiers."

Standing among the crowd, John Wilkes Booth remarked to his friends David Herold and Lewis Powell, "That means nigger citizenship. Now, by God, I will put him through. That will be the last speech he will ever make."

On the morning of April 14, the twenty-six-year-old Booth woke up in his hotel room hungover and depressed after another night of Washington's celebration of the defeat of the Confederacy.

Around noon, Booth was at nearby Ford's Theater to collect his mail when he heard the news that President Lincoln and the first lady would be attending that night's performance with their guests, Ulysses S. Grant and his wife, Julia.

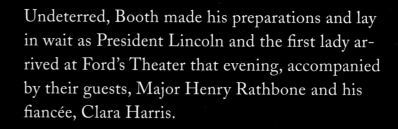

Undeterred, Booth made his preparations and lay in wait as President Lincoln and the first lady arrived at Ford's Theater that evening, accompanied by their guests, Major Henry Rathbone and his fiancée, Clara Harris.

The play that evening was the comedy, *Our American Cousin*. Booth knew the layout of Ford's and the timing of the play. As a famous actor, no one questioned his presence at the theater that night, and Booth found the door to the president's box unguarded.

Slipping inside unnoticed, Booth barricaded the door behind him with a wooden bar he had put in place earlier that day. He then waited for the end of the play's scene, knowing that it would leave only a single actor on the stage.

As the fifty-six-year-old president sat in a rocking chair next to his wife, Booth removed a single-shot pistol from his coat, cocked it, and took aim at the back of Lincoln's head.

You sockdologizing old man-trap!" were the last words Lincoln heard from the stage. As the crowd broke out in laughter, Booth pulled the trigger, and his bullet lodged itself deep inside Lincoln's brain.

Major Rathbone was the first to realize what was happening and rose to defend the president. Discarding the pistol, Booth drew a sharp hunting knife and lunged, dealing Rathbone a partially deflected blow that caused a deep cut from elbow to shoulder.

Booth then climbed the balustrade. As Rathbone reached for him and caught his coat, Booth leapt down onto the stage twelve feet below.

But the spur on Booth's boot caught on the corner of a framed portrait of George Washington, and he landed awkwardly, breaking his left leg just above the ankle.

Booth managed to rise to his feet and then triumphantly shouted the state motto of Virginia, "Sic semper tyrannis!" which in Latin means, "Thus always to tyrants!"

"The South is avenged." he added before running backstage, swinging wildly with his knife at anyone in his way. "I have done it!" Booth was heard to say as he made his escape.

Meanwhile, two of Booth's accomplices, the burly, tall, young veteran Confederate soldier, Lewis Powell, and a local assistant pharmacist named David Herold, were outside the home of Secretary of State William Seward.

Seward was already gravely injured from a near-fatal carriage accident just nine days earlier. With a metal apparatus holding his broken jaw in place, he lay recuperating in a bedroom on the third floor, attended to by his daughter Fanny and military nurse George Robinson.

Herold waited outside to guide their escape, but had prepared for Powell an authentic-looking medical delivery package. Powell told the young servant William Bell, who answered the front door, that he had come from Seward's doctor with medicine he must deliver to the secretary.

Though Bell repeatedly insisted that Powell leave the package with him, Powell pushed past him to the stairs, claiming it must be delivered in person. Minutes of bickering ensued, with Powell repeatedly saying, "I must go up."

At the top of the stairs, the Seward's son Frederick, who was his assistant secretary of state, confronted the stranger and told him to hand over the medicine or leave.

Powell relented, turning to leave, with Bell leading him toward the door.

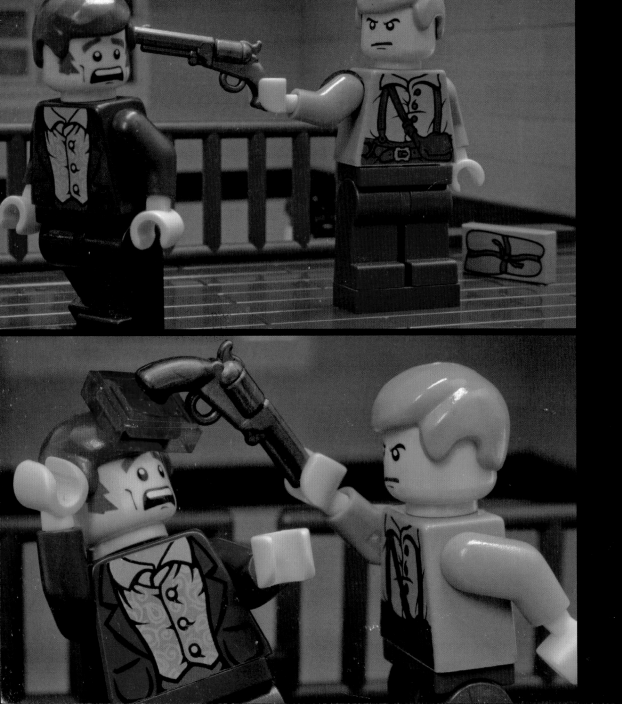

But suddenly, turning back toward Frederick Seward, Powell removed a revolver from his coat, aimed, and pulled the trigger. A click was heard, but the gun had misfired.

Powell then smashed his gun over Frederick Seward's head, managing to both break the gun and crack the younger Seward's skull in two places.

At this point William Bell ran out into the street for help, screaming, "Murder! Murder!" Fearing the plan was botched, Herold panicked and fled on his horse, leaving Powell to his own devices.

Powell took a knife from his coat and burst into the secretary of state's darkened bedroom, pushing his frail daughter Fanny out of the way, and hitting nurse Robinson in the forehead with his knife.

268676

He then lunged toward the helpless Seward, raising his knife over his head, and bringing it mightily down several times, attempting a death blow.

Seward was stabbed repeatedly in the neck and face before Robinson could jump on his back, preventing further attack on the elder Seward. Meanwhile, Fanny's continuous shrieks woke others in the house.

Another of Seward's sons joined Robinson in wrestling Powell out into the hallway. Powell stabbed Robinson twice deeply in the shoulder as Fanny and Seward's now awakened wife looked on in confusion and horror.

Finally, Powell struggled free and fled the house, shouting, "I'm mad! I'm mad!" Crossing paths with a State Department messenger who had just arrived at the house, Powell stabbed him in the back as he attempted to flee.

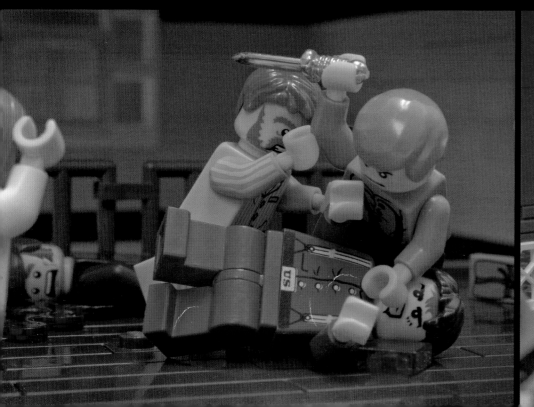

Powell mounted his horse and rode away, but he did not know his way around Washington, DC, without Herold as his guide and wound up spending the night in a cemetery.

Just after 10 PM, Booth's fourth accomplice, the carriage repairman George Atzerodt, was at the bar of the Kirkwood Hotel where both he and Vice President Andrew Johnson were staying. Atzerodt was attempting to work up the nerve to carry out his attack.

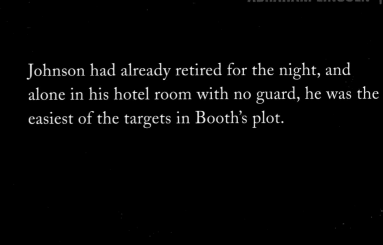

Johnson had already retired for the night, and alone in his hotel room with no guard, he was the easiest of the targets in Booth's plot.

But Atzerodt could not bring himself to do it, and he left the hotel to wander the streets of Washington for the next few hours.

For twelve days Booth and Herold evaded a massive manhunt but were finally tracked down by a Union cavalry unit as they hid in a tobacco barn twenty miles south of the Potomac River in Virginia.

Being a dark night, the soldiers could not see into the barn, so Booth was ordered to come out and surrender peacefully, or else they would burn down the barn.

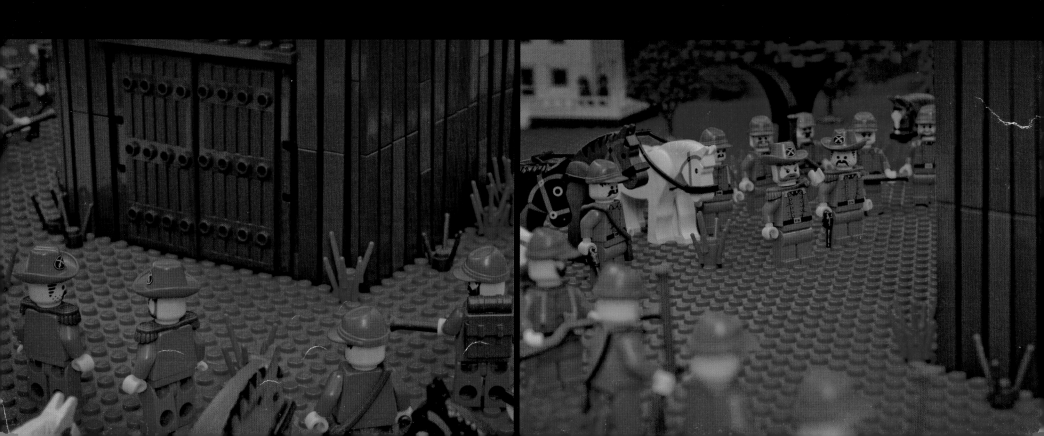

A panicked David Herold decided he did not wish to burn to death and came out of the barn unarmed to surrender. But Booth was defiant and remained inside with a broken leg and a stash of guns.

Captain, I consider you to be a brave and honorable man," Booth called out, "I am a cripple . . . If you'll take your men fifty yards from the door, I'll come out and fight you."

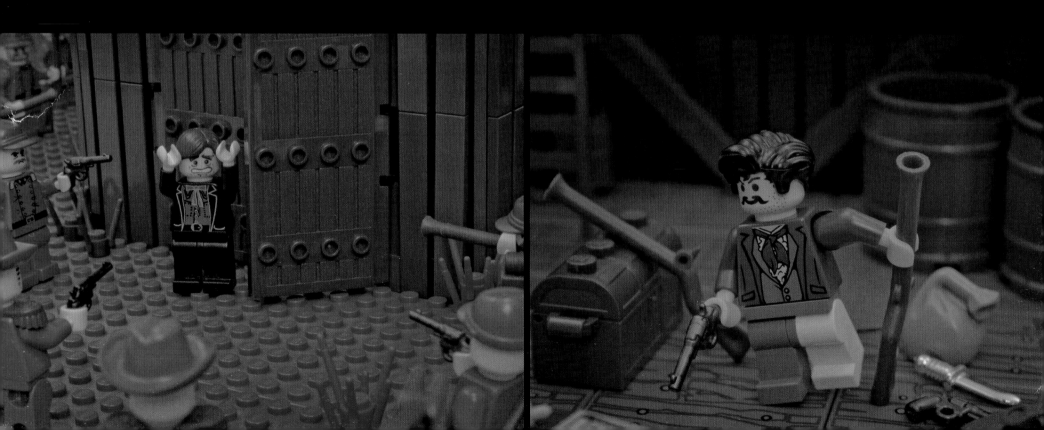

Having been given orders to capture Lincoln's assassin alive for questioning, they rebuffed his offer and lit the barn on fire, hoping to flush Booth out.

The heat inside the barn quickly grew intense, and Booth approached the back door of the barn using a crutch and holding his weapons. The light from the flames now allowed soldiers to see Booth through the cracks in the vertical planks of the barn.

A soldier named Boston Corbett took aim and shot Booth, hitting him in the neck, paralyzing him, and leaving him in excruciating pain. Later explaining to his superiors why he had shot Booth without orders, Corbett told them, "Providence directed me."

Seven years earlier, a deeply religious Boston Corbett had decided to take Jesus's direction in Matthew 19:12 to heart. To avoid the temptations of prostitutes, he had cut off his own testicles with a knife.

He then went to a prayer meeting and ate a hearty meal before seeking medical attention.

Booth was taken to the front porch of the nearby farmhouse, where, barely able to speak, he whispered, "Tell mother, I died for my country." He then looked down at his hands and uttered in his dying breath, "Useless . . . useless . . ."

After several months, William Seward and his son Frederick both made full recoveries. The elder Seward, with his face now permanently scarred, continued in his role as secretary of state under President Andrew Johnson, and in 1867, arranged the purchase of Alaska from Russia for $7.2 million.

For the rest of his life, Major Henry Rathbone was haunted by his inability to prevent Lincoln's assassination. On December 23, 1883, he shot his wife Clara to death and attempted to commit suicide with a knife. He survived, but spent the remainder of his days in an insane asylum.

Chapter 4
JAMES A. GARFIELD
July 2, 1881

Born in Illinois in 1841, Charles Julius Guiteau was raised by his poor, intensely religious father after his mother died when he was seven years old. Young Julius, as he was known, was a precocious reader and writer.

In his late teens, he decided to be known by his first name Charles, claiming that Julius "had too much of the Negro about it." He used some inheritance money to enroll at the University of Michigan at Ann Arbor.

At age eighteen, at the insistence of his father who disapproved of secular education, Guiteau left the University of Michigan to join the Oneida Religious Commune in Upstate New York.

Among the community's beliefs was that multiple sex partners was morally superior to monogamy and that to avoid "the horrors and the fear of involuntary propagation," males should master the technique of having sex without ejaculating.

Though the practice of free love had attracted Guiteau to the community, he consistently found his amorous advances rebuffed by the women at Oneida, who did not share his grandiose opinion of himself and who nicknamed him "Charles Git-Out."

Believing himself chosen by God for a greater purpose, Guiteau left Oneida at age twenty-three and moved to New York City with confidence that he would soon achieve riches and fame as the publisher of a new major newspaper called the *Daily Theocrat*.

Over the next few months, Guiteau arranged numerous meetings with potential backers and advertisers, who scoffed at him and found his religious views that he had adopted from Oneida peculiar, such as the belief that the Second Coming of Christ had occurred in AD 70.

Giving up on the newspaper business, Guiteau next set out to practice law. Passing a lax bar exam, he set up a practice in Chicago, where during trials he would reportedly "talk and act like a crazy man" with long digressions concerning theology and divinity.

After fourteen financially unrewarding years as a lawyer, continuously borrowing money from friends and relatives, and incurring mountains of unpaid debts, Guiteau was inspired to write a book about his own religious revelations called *The Truth: A Companion to The Bible.*

Unable to convince a publisher to give his work an audience, Guiteau set out with great enthusiasm on an evangelical lecture tour. Traveling from city to city, he would rent out church halls and charge people 25 cents to hear him speak. His audiences were rarely more than a handful, and he was often ridiculed.

While traveling, Guiteau habitually rode trains without paying any fare and would sneak out of hotels and boarding houses before paying the bill. This behavior eventually caught up with him, and he spent a short amount of time in jail in New York City.

Guiteau next became intensely interested in politics, and during the election of 1880, he wrote a speech in support of the Civil War hero and respected congressman, James A. Garfield, which he managed to deliver only once, in truncated form, at a small political rally.

Once Garfield was elected, Guiteau believed it only a matter of time before he would be justly rewarded. He wrote letters to Garfield suggesting himself for the consulship to Paris, and traveled to Washington, DC, to join the throngs of office seekers at the White House, each day hoping to gain an audience with the president.

Turned away from the White House, Guiteau began pestering people at the State Department on a daily basis until Secretary of State James G. Blaine himself told Guiteau that Blaine would not consider him for any appointment, and to "never speak about the Paris consulship to me again."

While in Washington, Guiteau kept up with the latest political news in the papers and became increasingly concerned about Garfield's struggle for power with Senator Roscoe Conkling and his faction of the Republican Party known as "the Stalwarts."

Believing the rift to be a grave danger to the health of the Republican Party, it was in this mindset that on May 18, 1881, while laying in bed, Guiteau first had this thought: "If the president were out of the way, everything would go better." He soon came to believe God had given him a mission.

On June 8, 1881, Guiteau borrowed $15 from an acquaintance and bought himself a pistol, taking care to choose one that looked impressive, believing it would soon be on display in a museum.

Having never owned or fired a gun in his life, Guiteau went down to the banks of the Potomac to practice shooting at the river and at trees.

Guiteau stalked the president for days, eventually following Garfield and the first lady to church. He determined to kill him there, thinking, "There could not possibly be a better place to remove a man than at his devotions."

As the president and his wife were listening to the sermon, Guiteau noticed an open window that would give him an easy shot at Garfield without accidentally injuring others.

But the sermon being given was not to Guiteau's liking, and unable to contain himself, he blurted aloud, "What think ye of Christ?" That night in his diary, the president made note of a "dull young man, with a loud voice" who had interrupted the pastor.

Before getting another chance the next Sunday, Guiteau read in the paper that Garfield would be taking his ailing wife to the New Jersey shore to recuperate. Determining when their train would leave, Guiteau lay in wait at the Baltimore and Potomac train station.

But the sight of the enfeebled first lady clinging to the president caused Guiteau to hesitate, and the president and his wife walked past Guiteau without noticing him.

When Garfield returned to Washington at the end of the month, Guiteau took to simply waiting for him on a bench outside the White House.

On the evening of July 1, Garfield exited the White House and went on a walk with Secretary of State Blaine. Guiteau followed them, gun in hand.

Although he did not take the opportunity to attack either man, Guiteau was outraged by the warm friendship on display between the president and the man who had personally rebuffed him, and he determined that the next time there would be no hesitation.

That night, Guiteau stayed at the posh Riggs Hotel where Garfield had stayed before his inauguration. The next morning, he ate a large breakfast and charged it to his room, never intending to pay, as was his custom.

Before leaving the hotel, Guiteau wrote a note he then put in his pocket. "The President's tragic death was a sad necessity," it read, "but it will unite the Republican Party and save the Republic. I presume the President was a Christian and that he will be happier in paradise than here."

He then walked to the train station, where once again the president was expected to arrive any moment, this time to embark on a vacation, reunite with his wife, and attend his college reunion in Massachusetts.

At 9.30 AM, Garfield arrived at the station accompanied by Secretary of State Blaine and the president's two teenage sons, Henry and Jim. They walked right past Guiteau.

This time, Guiteau did not hesitate. He drew his pistol and with a look of determination fired from three feet away. The bullet passed through Garfield's right arm and then hit the toolbox of a workman.

Garfield threw his arms upward and cried out, "My God! What is this?"

Now panicking, Guiteau fired again, hitting Garfield in the back. This bullet missed the spine and vital organs, but fractured two ribs and came to rest just behind his pancreas.

The president collapsed to the ground. Guiteau put his gun in his pocket and attempted to leave but was quickly apprehended by the crowd.

As an angry mob began to shout, "Lynch him! policemen quickly removed Guiteau from the station as he shouted, "I am a stalwart of the Stalwarts! I did it and I want to be arrested! Arthur is president now!"

In the carriage ride to police headquarters, Guiteau claimed to be good friends with Vice President Chester Arthur and said to the detective sitting next to him that if he were to assure Guiteau a choice jail cell, he would have him made chief of police.

Conscious, but in excruciating pain, Garfield was taken to an upstairs room at the station, where a series of doctors used their fingers and other unsterilized probes to search for the bullet.

Abraham Lincoln's son, Robert Todd Lincoln, serving as Garfield's secretary of war, was present at the train station, and remarked, "How many hours of sorrow I have passed in this town."

Garfield was moved to the White House, where for weeks on end he was treated by doctors disdainful and dismissive of germ theory and the sorts of antiseptic medical procedures that had, by this point, become commonplace in Europe. Consequently, the president's injuries festered and become severely infected.

To help locate the bullet still lodged in Garfield's back, Alexander Graham Bell invented the first metal detector. The doctor in charge, however, only used the device to search the side of the body where he incorrectly presumed the bullet had come to rest.

In jail, giving interviews with the press, Guiteau expressed his certainty that the American people were on his side and that Chester Arthur would soon pardon him without a trial. He made plans for a speaking tour that would he would embark on that fall and for his own eventual run for the presidency in 1884.

Guiteau offered his autobiography to the *New York Herald* and tacked on to the end of it a personal ad indicating that he was looking to marry "an elegant Christian lady of wealth, under 30, belonging to a first-class family."

Unable to keep food down, Garfield lost seventy-five pounds. In September, the president was moved to the Jersey Shore to avoid the stifling heat of Washington, DC. His body now racked with infectious disease, the forty-nine-year-old president died on September 19, 1881.

"Oh! Why am I made to suffer this cruel wrong!" said First Lady Lucretia Garfield over her husband's body. It is widely believed that with modern medical practices, Garfield would have recovered from his injuries within weeks.

At Guiteau's trial, he compared his own patriotic heroism to George Washington and Ulysses S. Grant. He maintained that God had compelled him to "remove" President Garfield and that nothing that God commands can violate any law.

Guiteau's brother-in-law acted as his defense lawyer but was continually berated by his own client with outbursts such as, "You are a jackass on the question of cross-examination. I must tell you that right in public, to your face."

Flabbergasted to be found guilty and sentenced to hang, Guiteau spent his last days writing warnings to President Arthur (who failed to pardon him) that he would burn in hell, and that God would "get even" with the American people for killing God's man as he had with the Jews when they killed Jesus.

Standing on the gallows, Guiteau recited a last poem he had written, called, "I Am Going to the Lordy." "I saved my party and my land, Glory Hallelujah!" said Guiteau. "But they have murdered me for it, and that is the reason I am going to the Lordy."

"Glory, glory, glory" were Charles Julius Guiteau's last words before he gave a signal to the hangman to drop the trap door, causing him to fall to his death on June 30, 1882.

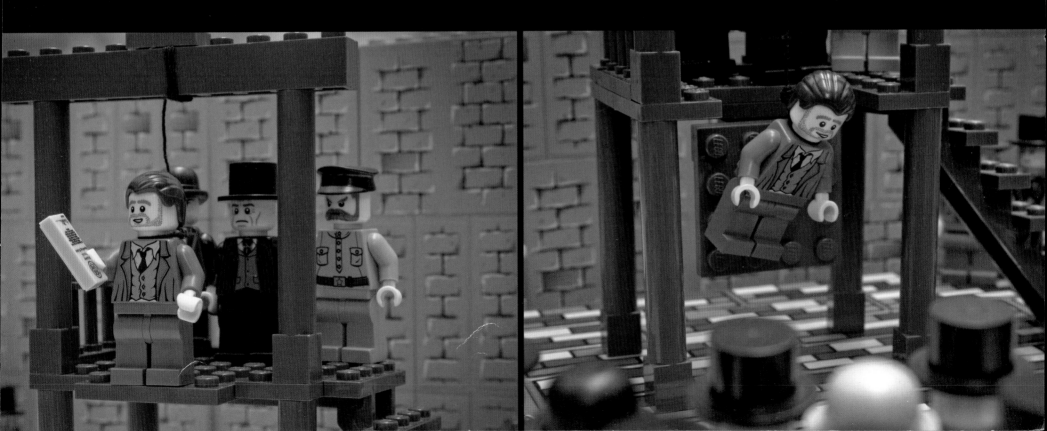

Chapter 5
WILLIAM MCKINLEY
September 6, 1901

Millions of Americans flocked to the Pan-American Exposition of 1901, held in Buffalo, New York. It was a chance for Americans to experience other cultures at exhibits like the mock Japanese village, the "Darkest Africa" exhibit, and a display of Indian "savages."

It was also a chance to see demonstrations of the latest technological marvels, including improved phonographs, motion picture mutoscopes, x-ray devices, and a machine called the electrograph, which could transmit pictures across telegraph wires.

Furthermore, it was a chance to experience the strange and the exotic, including an elephant that the British military had used in Afghanistan, and a "Trip to the Moon" exhibit in which midgets with spikes on their backs danced and handed out green cheese.

The popular, recently reelected President William McKinley visited the exposition on September 5, 1901, and delivered what was considered one of the best speeches of his career to a crowd of over 50,000.

The next day, the president visited Niagara Falls and was scheduled to return to the expo for a public reception at 4 PM. Nervous about security, the president's secretary twice urged him to cancel the event. "Why should I?" McKinley responded. "No one would wish to hurt me."

As thousands waited in line for a chance to shake hands with the president, McKinley's security men kept their eye on a suspicious-looking, dark-haired man with a moustache.

When the swarthy man reached the front of the line, he clasped the president's hand for an oddly long period of time. Finally, one of the security men stepped forward to intervene and move the man along.

Noticing that the next man in line had a bandaged right hand, McKinley offered him his left hand to shake.

But this man did not want to shake the president's hand. Instead, he shot him twice in the chest with a revolver concealed by the white handkerchief wrapped around his hand.

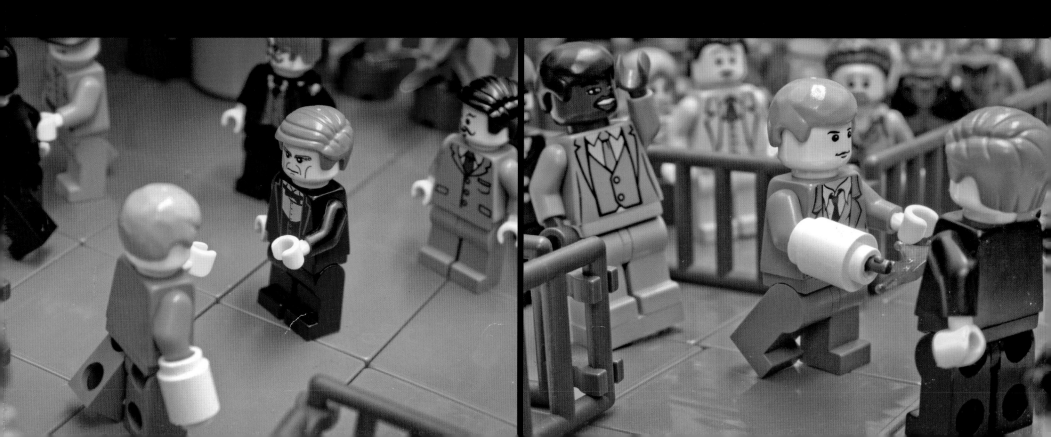

McKinley started to fall backward but was caught by his security men. Thinking quickly, James Parker, the man waiting in line behind the assassin, punched the gunman in the neck, stopping him from getting off a third shot.

Realizing what had happened, the crowd began to viciously pummel the assassin. He would likely have been killed on the spot but that the seriously wounded president was heard to say, "Don't let them hurt him. . . . Go easy on him, boys."

Abraham Lincoln's son Robert Todd Lincoln had been personally invited by McKinley to the Pan-American Exposition and was just arriving when the president was shot. He was later quoted as saying that he would no longer accept invitations from presidents, as "there is a certain fatality to presidential functions when I am present."

McKinley was taken to the exposition hospital. There, a surgeon named Dr. Matthew Mann, who was considered a leading authority on gynecology, but who had little experience with gunshot wounds, operated on the president, suturing his perforated stomach, but was unable to find one of the two bullets.

Nonetheless, Mann was convinced McKinley would make a full recovery—so much so, that the next day he returned to the barbershop to finish getting a haircut that had been interrupted by the news that the president had been shot.

Vice President Theodore Roosevelt told reporters, "I am absolutely sure the president will recover," and then left with his family for a vacation in the Adirondack Mountains, not bothering to keep himself near telephone or telegraph lines for updates on the president's condition.

Inventor Thomas Edison sent his latest, most advanced x-ray machine to Buffalo, hoping it could find the bullet still lodged inside McKinley. But when it arrived, it was missing a key part and, therefore, could not be used.

On September 13, things took a sudden turn for the worse. Unknown to the doctors caring for him, gangrene had set in on the president's internal wounds. By day's end, the fifty-eight-year-old president, aware that he was dying, said, "It is useless, gentlemen. I think we ought to have prayer."

First Lady Ida McKinley, who had been struggling with her own illness for years, sobbed over him, saying, "I want to go too. I want to go too." The president replied, "We are all going. We are all going. God's will be done, not ours." He died in the early morning of September 14, the eighth day after having been shot.

At police headquarters, the twenty-eight-year-old Leon Czolgosz gave a full confession. "I am an anarchist," he said. "I don't believe we should have any rulers. It is right to kill them . . . I fully understood what I was doing when I shot the president . . . I don't regret my act, because I was doing what I could for the great cause."

Czolgosz further explained his motive. "McKinley was going around the country shouting prosperity when there was no prosperity for the poor man . . . I didn't believe one man should have so much and another should have none."

Born in 1873, near Detroit, Michigan, to a poor family of Prussian immigrants, Czolgosz began supplementing his family's income at age six, shining shoes and delivering papers. His mother died in childbirth when he was ten years old.

At age fourteen, Czolgosz began working ten- and twelve-hour shifts at a glass factory, working in dangerous conditions with red hot glass. His position at that age was not unusual. By the turn of the century there were 284,000 children in the United States between the ages of ten and fifteen working in mills, factories, and mines.

The government-aided rise of national corporations saw vast wealth concentrated among a small number of captains of finance and industry, while by the end of the 1880s, 40 percent of the workforce lived below the poverty level. When unions were formed and strikes called, workers would be routinely fired en masse and put on blacklists to prevent them from being hired again.

In such conditions, national unions formed, and mass strikes to protest long hours and cuts to already low wages became increasingly common. Corporate bosses would hire their own private security forces to ensure that strikers could not shut down production during strikes.

When private security was not enough, local police were called upon but often sided with the striking workers. Government militias would then be brought in from other areas and, in heated confrontations, violence erupted and crowds were fired on.

Many were killed or wounded. The notorious industrialist Jay Gould once boasted, "I can hire one-half of the working class to kill the other."

After striking and being subsequently fired and blacklisted from his new job at a wire mill in Cleveland, Ohio, Czolgosz prayed to God for help, but believing his prayers fell on deaf ears, he turned to socialist and anarchist writings that seemed to offer solutions to the problems of the working man in this lifetime.

Over the next few years, Czolgosz attended many socialist political meetings in Cleveland and was mesmerized when he heard a speech by the fiery spokeswoman for anarchism, Emma Goldman.

Though she did not support the use of violence to achieve anarchist goals, she could not condemn those who were willing to sacrifice their own life for their ideals and had praised the Italian-American anarchist who had recently assassinated the hated King Umberto I of Italy.

Hoping to do something for the cause, Czolgosz went to Chicago and tried to make connections with Goldman's anarchist friends. In doing so, he mentioned to one person his disillusionment with the McKinley administration, in particular the outrages committed in the Philippine Islands by the American government.

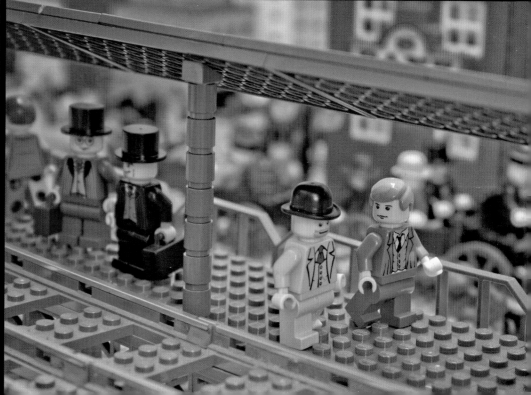

Having "liberated" the Philippines from Spain in the brief Spanish-American War, the Americans immediately declared the Filipinos unfit for self-rule, and when the Filipinos established their own government anyhow, the United States sent in tens of thousands of troops.

The native population fighting for independence was labeled as insurgents, and in their war to establish control of the Philippines, American soldiers burned down whole villages and massacred men, women, and children, with a death toll of hundreds of thousands.

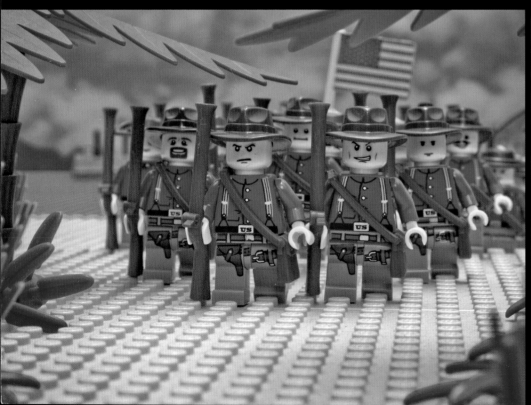

But Czolgosz's overeagerness and questions about what plans of action the anarchists were drawing up made Emma Goldman's friends suspicious of him, and an ad was placed in the major anarchist newspaper of the time warning others that a spy was in their midst.

In late August of 1901, Czolgosz was in Chicago when he saw in a newspaper that President McKinley would be attending the Pan-American Exposition in Buffalo. He purchased a train ticket to Buffalo that same day.

The day before the president arrived, Czolgosz went into a hardware store and purchased a .32 caliber Iver Johnson revolver.

Nine days after McKinley died, Czolgosz's trial was held and took only eight hours. He did not speak a word at the trial save for his plea: "Guilty." His defense attorneys spent more time praising McKinley than defending their client. The jury sentenced him to death.

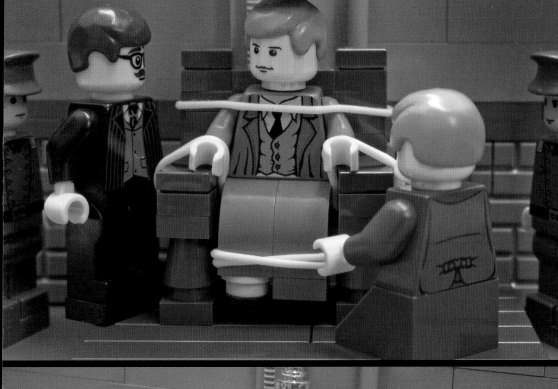

Just over a month later, Czolgosz was brought to the electric chair at Auburn Prison. Once strapped in, he declared, "I killed the president for the good of the laboring people, the good people. I am not sorry for my crime."

The full current of 1,700 volts was then sent through his body for forty-five seconds, and Leon Czolgosz was dead.

Chapter 6

THEODORE ROOSEVELT
October 14, 1912

When William McKinley died, Theodore Roosevelt was sworn in, becoming, at age forty-two, the youngest US president ever. While in office, he moved his Republican Party in the direction of progressivism, breaking up corporate monopolies and regulating businesses with the passage of the Meat Inspection Act and the Pure Food and Drug Act.

After winning election to a second term by a wide majority in 1904, Roosevelt chose not to run for a third term. Instead, he supported his friend William Howard Taft, and then departed for an extended African safari in which he and his companions hunted and trapped thousands of animals, large and small.

In 1912, however, Roosevelt returned to politics, forming the Progressive Party, which was popularly known as the Bull Moose Party. He ran for a third term as president, challenging his former friend Taft and Democratic candidate Woodrow Wilson. Roosevelt traveled around the country giving up to thirty speeches per day.

The strain on his throat was considerable. While in Milwaukee on October 14, Roosevelt's doctor, Scurry Terrell, tried in vain to get him to rest rather than meet for dinner with party supporters at the Hotel Gilpatrick before delivering a speech that night.

Just after 8 PM, Roosevelt exited the hotel and was greeted by the cheers of hundreds who had gathered on the sidewalk and street. Accompanied by local party leader Henry Cochems and some staff, the former president strode quickly toward his waiting automobile.

Before seating himself, Roosevelt held his hat aloft to acknowledge the crowd. Just then, a thirty-six-year-old man named John Schrank reached his arm out between two bystanders and fired a revolver at Roosevelt, hitting him in the chest.

Schrank was immediately knocked to the ground as the crowd began to shout, "Lynch him! Kill him!" Roosevelt, momentarily knocked into his seat, but then able to stand, commanded, "Don't hurt him. Bring him here. I want to see him."

Taking Schrank's head in his hands, Roosevelt said to his would-be assassin, "What did you do it for?"

Seeing only a dull-eyed, expressionless face looking back at him, an exasperated Roosevelt said,
"Oh, what's the use? Turn him over to the police,"
and Schrank was taken away.

"He plinked me, Henry," Roosevelt said to Cochems, noticing blood spreading out on his shirt.
The bullet had been partially deflected by the
metal glasses case in Roosevelt's jacket pocket before lodging in his chest. By this time, Dr. Terrell
had arrived and pleaded for Roosevelt to immediately go to a hospital.

Roosevelt removed a folded fifty-page speech from his jacket pocket and saw that the bullet had passed through it, leaving two holes. He then proceeded to speak for ninety minutes in support of the Progressive platform, including the establishment of laws prohibiting child labor and a law establishing a minimum wage for women.

While in custody, Schrank spoke openly about his motives. He believed he was God's instrument and that it was right to kill any man who seeks a third term in office. He compared himself to Moses and Joan of Arc—as others who were called to act by God.

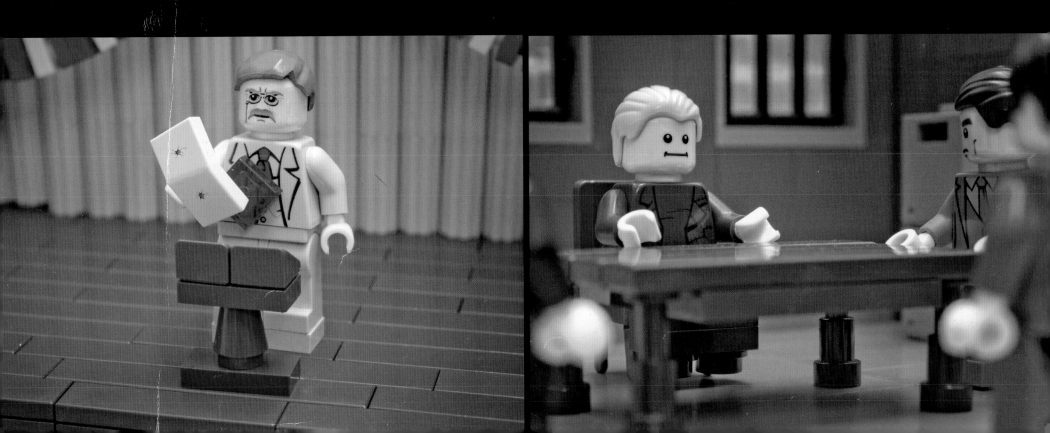

Convinced he would one day be seen as a hero, Schrank requested his gun and the bullet that struck Roosevelt be given to the New York Historical Society. Informed that doctors decided to leave the bullet lodged in Roosevelt's chest, he got upset and said, "That's my bullet!"

Schrank told police that back in 1901, the night after William McKinley died, he had a dream in which the deceased president sat up in his coffin and pointed to a man in a monk's outfit whom he recognized as Theodore Roosevelt. "This is my murderer," said McKinley. "Avenge my death."

John Schrank had come to America from Germany at age twelve and lived with his uncle and aunt, who owned and operated a neighborhood saloon in New York City. Schrank was well mannered and helped tend bar and performed other chores.

When his uncle and aunt died, they left the business to their nephew, who promptly sold it and lived off of the profit. Shrank spent much of his time on walks around the city, writing poetry or jotting down ideas in a notebook.

Schrank once wrote an essay about four pillars of the US government: that no man should run for a third term as president; that the United States should engage in no wars of conquest; that the Monroe Doctrine must be upheld; and that all presidents should be Protestant (despite that Schrank himself was Catholic).

When he learned that Roosevelt was seeking the nomination of his party for a third term in August of 1912, Schrank was outraged. Then, on the night of September 13, while writing a poem, Schrank heard a voice: "Let no murderer occupy the presidential chair for a third term. Avenge my death!" Turning, he saw the visage of a ghostlike President McKinley.

Convinced that most Americans shared his conviction about would-be "third termers," Schrank later told police he was surprised no one else had sought to stop Roosevelt before he did. As an unmarried man with no children, though, Schrank figured he might as well be the one to act. He went out the next day and purchased a .38 caliber Colt revolver.

In his attempts to get close enough to Roosevelt, Schrank followed him on the campaign trail, traveling through Charlestown, Augusta, Atlanta, Birmingham, Chattanooga, Nashville, Louisville, Evansville, Chicago, and finally, Milwaukee.

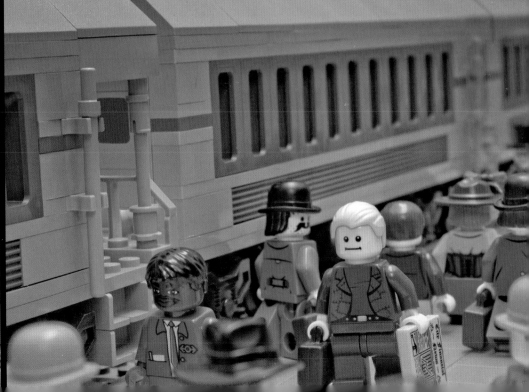

Around 7 PM on October 14, Schrank entered a saloon, bought the musicians there a round of drinks, and asked them to play "The Star-Spangled Banner." He smiled and danced around a bit as they played. He treated them to a second round of drinks, then left the saloon just minutes before shooting Roosevelt.

A team of five psychiatrists determined that John Schrank was insane and not fit for trial. Upon hearing this, Schrank thanked each of the doctors, shook their hands, and told them that while he disagreed with their diagnosis, he felt they had done their best.

This polite and genial attitude continued the rest of his life. Schrank was committed to a prison hospital at Waupon, Wisconsin, where he was considered a model patient and nicknamed "Uncle John." In thirty-one years there, he never received a visitor or letter. He died in 1943, at age sixty-seven.

Roosevelt recovered quickly. With votes split between the Progressives for Roosevelt and the Republicans for Taft, they both lost out to Democrat Woodrow Wilson, who won the presidency with only 42 percent of the popular vote.

The bullet would stay in Roosevelt's chest the
rest of his life, where he claimed it never bothered
him. After the election, the former president and
his son Kermit embarked on an expedition to ex-
plore the River of Doubt in the Brazilian jungle.

Chapter 7
FRANKLIN D. ROOSEVELT
February 15, 1933

Giuseppe Zangara was born in 1900 in southern Italy. His mother died when he was two years old, and his father was often abusive to him. Removing him from school at age six after only two months, his father put him to work at hard labor, carrying bricks and tiles.

Zangara grew to be only five feet tall, weighing 105 pounds. In his midteens he joined the Italian army but hated military life. By this point he had developed severe stomach pains that would cause him misery throughout his life.

By the end of his service, he blamed capitalists and corrupt government for his plight and decided he would kill Italy's King Victor Emmanuel III. Taking a pistol to a railroad depot, Zangara's plot was thwarted when he could not get close enough to see the king over the tall guards in front of him.

Zangara then moved to the United States to live with an uncle in Paterson, New Jersey, and found work as a bricklayer. In 1929, he became a US citizen so that he would be eligible to join a union. He lived a solitary life and did not smoke, drink, date, or even socialize with others.

Despite the onset of the Great Depression, Zangara saved enough money to travel briefly to both Los Angeles and Panama. He then settled in Miami, where he occasionally supplemented his savings by betting on dog or horse races.

But nothing in life eased his constant suffering, and by early February 1933, running low on money, Zangara decided he'd had enough. He bought a gun in a pawnshop and decided he would go to Washington, DC, and kill President Herbert Hoover.

The next day, however, he noticed in a newspaper that Franklin Delano Roosevelt, who had just beaten Hoover in the election of 1932, would be making a speech in Miami the very next day. He altered his plans, later commenting on this decision: "Hoover and Roosevelt—everybody the same."

Zangara managed to get as close as the third row, about twenty-five feet away. Standing on a wobbly folding chair, he barely had time to aim his revolver before Roosevelt's 135-word speech concluded. Holding his arm over the heads of those in front of him, Zangara fired five shots in rapid succession.

Six people were injured by Zangara's bullets, including Chicago Mayor Anton Cermak, but Roosevelt himself was unscathed. In a scene of chaos, Zangara was tackled and beaten by bystanders as the president-elect attempted to get the wounded Cermak in the car and drive to the hospital.

At Dade County Jail, the sheriff questioned Zangara about his motives, asking what he thought of anarchism. "Foolishness," he replied. Asked about socialism, communism, and fascism, "More foolishness," said Zangara. He also rejected religion. "I don't believe in nothing," he told police.

Zangara was brought to trial four days later on four accounts of attempted murder. In his heavily accented, imperfect English, he pled guilty, saying, "I decided to kill and make him suffer . . . I get even with capitalists by kill the president. My stomach hurt long time." Asked if he was sorry for what he did, "Sure," he replied. "Sorry I no kill him."

He was quickly sentenced to eighty years of hard labor in prison by Judge E. C. Collins. On hearing this, Zangara said to Collins, "Oh, Judge, don't be stingy! Give me hundred years!"

When Mayor Cermak died of complications from his bullet wound, Zangara was brought back to court and, after a brief trial, was sentenced to death. "You give me electric chair. I'm no afraid that chair," Zangara responded to the judge. "You're one of the capitalists. You crook man, too. Put me in electric chair, I no care."

Judge Uly Thompson took the opportunity to urge the US Congress to pass legislation to outlaw and confiscate all handguns. "It is a ridiculous state of society," he stated, "that an assassin may be permitted to arm himself and go at liberty throughout the land killing whom he will kill."

On March 20, just thirty-three days after the shootings, Giuseppe Zangara was led to "Old Sparky," the electric chair at Florida State Prison at Raiford. Seeing members of the press snapping photos, Zangara rebuked them: "No take picture! Capitalists! Lousy, dirty capitalist!"

"Goodbye to poor people everywhere! . . . Pusha da button!" said Zangara, just before the lethal dose of electricity was applied. "Go ahead, pusha da button!"

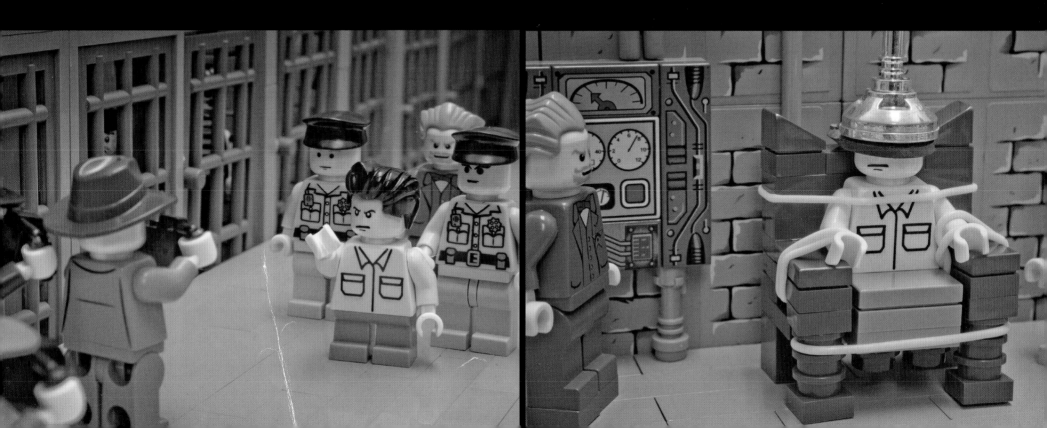

Chapter 8

JOHN F. KENNEDY
December 11, 1960

In 1960, Richard Pavlick was a seventy-three-year-old retired postal worker from Belmont, New Hampshire, with two missing fingers on his right hand. He lived alone and was considered a local eccentric who wrote frequent "rambling and dumb" letters to newspapers and was vocal at town meetings.

Virulently anti-Catholic, Pavlick hated John F. Kennedy. When Richard Nixon lost to Kennedy by the narrowest of margins in the 1960 election, Pavlick told people that life had lost all meaning to him. He talked of destroying himself and taking others with him. "He was always rambling about something," noted a neighbor.

During the last week of November, Pavlick sold his house, donating the money to a local youth center. He then set off in his 1950 Buick and began stalking the president-elect at the Kennedy family mansion in Hyannis Port, Massachusetts.

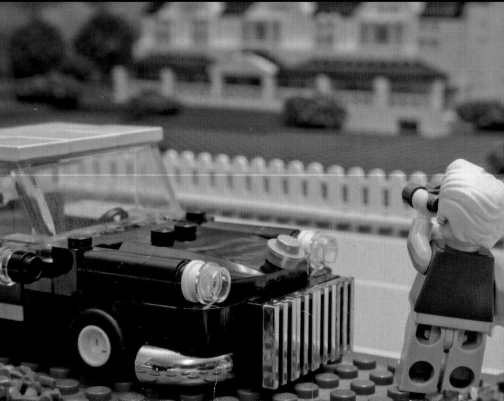

Pavlick returned to Belmont and mentioned to Postmaster Thomas Murphy that he had been to Hyannis Port and that secret service agents are stupid. Murphy was busy at the time and didn't think much of it, but later wondered why a man who hated Kennedy would travel to Hyannis Port to see him.

In early December, Pavlick continued to stalk Kennedy, driving to Washington, DC, and then on to Palm Beach, Florida, where the Kennedys had a winter home. At some point along the way, he stopped and purchased ten sticks of dynamite, four large canisters of gasoline, detonators, and wiring.

On the morning of Sunday, December 11, Pavlick sat in his dynamite-laden car with a trigger in hand and waited for the president-elect to emerge from his vacation home to head to church.

His plan was to drive directly at Kennedy's car and then detonate his car bomb at the last moment, killing his target and himself. But when Pavlick saw that Kennedy's wife and two young children had come outside to see him off, he chose to wait for a more opportune time to act.

Following him to church, Pavlick concealed a stick of dynamite under his coat and attempted to approach Kennedy during the mass, but Secret Service Agent Gerald Blaine noticed him getting too close to the president-elect and quietly guided him out of the church.

Meanwhile, back in New Hampshire, Postmaster Murphy had become suspicious when cryptic postcards he received from Pavlick mentioned that he would soon hear from him "in a big way." Noticing the postmarks were from cities Kennedy frequented, he contacted the Secret Service.

Kennedy left town the next day but was due to return to Palm Beach on December 16. On the 15th, however, Pavlick was pulled over for a minor traffic violation. Seven sticks of dynamite were found in his car, and Pavlick was arrested.

"I believe that the Kennedys bought the presidency and the White House," Pavlick told police. Before Kennedy could become president, Pavlick said he intended to "remove him in the only way it was available to me."

fined to mental hospitals for six years. Upon release, he lived in Manchester, New Hampshire, where he was often seen wearing a sandwich board in public, holding a petition for a public hearing to clear his name. He died in 1975, at age eighty-eight.

Chapter 9

JOHN F. KENNEDY
November 22, 1963

Lee Harvey Oswald was born in 1939, two months after his father's death. During his early years, Oswald and his mother moved between New Orleans, Fort Worth, and the Bronx. At age fourteen, he was caught skipping school while wandering the Bronx Zoo.

Taken for psychological assessment, doctors noted Oswald had compensatory fantasies of omnipotence and killing people. He scored a well above average IQ of 118, and one social worker noted "a rather pleasant, appealing quality about this emotionally-starved, affectionless youngster."

In New York City, Oswald had his first exposure to Marxism, being handed a flyer protesting the execution of Julius and Ethel Rosenberg for supplying nuclear secrets to the Soviet Union. An avid reader, Oswald spent much of his time in high school reading the works of Karl Marx and Friedrich Engels.

Wanting to follow in his older brother's footsteps and to escape his overbearing mother, Oswald joined the US Marines as soon as he reached the eligibility age of seventeen. In training he learned to use a rifle to hit targets up to 500 yards away, becoming a certified sharpshooter.

He also trained to become a radar surveillance specialist and was shipped off to Atsugi, Japan, where he worked as a military aircraft controller at a hub for the high altitude U-2 planes used to spy on the Soviets. His superiors praised his performance.

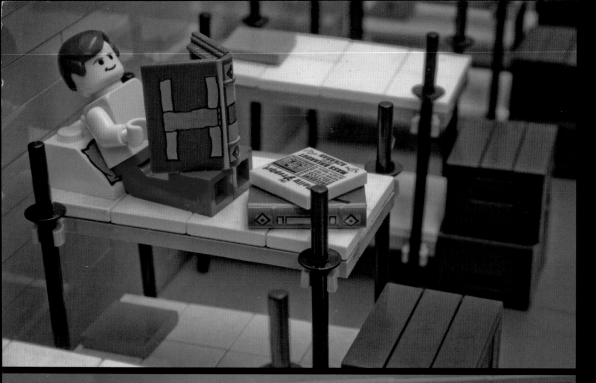

In his downtime, Oswald did not join his fellow marines on their excursions into Tokyo in search of beer and women but instead read books like Orwell's *1984*, Whitman's *Leaves of Grass*, and taught himself to speak Russian with rudimentary fluency.

While in Japan, Oswald had his first sexual experience, hiring an expensive prostitute. Then one day in the barracks he shot himself in the left arm when he accidentally dropped a pistol he had mail-ordered and was carrying without authorization.

Oswald was subsequently court-martialed, demoted, and spent seventeen humiliating days in the brig. After a stint in Taiwan and the Philippines, he was put on janitorial duty for the last months of his enlistment. Meanwhile, he began to idealize life in the Soviet Union and made plans to defect.

Upon receiving his honorable discharge from the Marines, Oswald set off on a passenger liner to France, took a boat across the channel to England, and then a plane to Finland, where he arranged for a seven-day visa to the Soviet Union. Taking a train across the border he arrived in Moscow just three days before his twentieth birthday.

A tour guide was assigned to him by the government, and Oswald told her of his wish to become
a Soviet citizen. In a written statement, Oswald
stated, "I am a communist and a worker and I have
lived in a decadent capitalist society where the
workers are slaves."

Oswald was put up in a hotel room while waiting to hear back about his request for Soviet citizenship. During this time, he practiced his Russian and wrote to his brother, saying he would "never return to the United States, which is a country I hate."

But when his weeklong visa expired, Oswald was informed he must return to the United States. Unable to handle this unexpected rejection, Oswald filled the bathtub and slit his wrist. He was found by his tour guide and rushed to a hospital.

After a week of recovery in the hospital, Oswald marched into the American Embassy, turned in his passport, and renounced his American citizenship. He further threatened to pass on to the Soviets any and all military information he acquired as a radar technician for the US Marines.

The Soviets did not offer citizenship to Oswald, but they did supply him with foreign residence documents and sent him 400 miles away to Minsk to work at a radio and TV factory. He was given a very large apartment by Russian standards and a salary about twice what his coworkers received.

Popular with the ladies from the local college, Oswald had several brief flings before falling madly in love with foreign language student Ella Germann. When she rebuffed him, Oswald was devastated. To get back at her, Oswald immediately began dating, and three weeks later married, the nineteen-year-old pharmacy student Marina Prusakova.

Oswald grew tired of Soviet life after a year, and attempted to patch up relations with the American Embassy so he could return to the United States. Another year and a half passed as the Americans and Soviets decided how to handle the situation. Oswald's first daughter, June, was born a few months before he and his family were allowed to come to the United States.

Settling in Fort Worth, Texas, Oswald worked a series of menial jobs to support his family. Speaking only Russian at home, he discouraged Marina from learning English. The marriage quickly soured. Marina routinely berated Oswald, and Oswald often struck back with physical abuse.

Now disenchanted with the Soviets' overly bureaucratic form of communism, Oswald began to idealize Fidel Castro's Cuba and began his attempts to build his credentials as a Marxist revolutionary. He mail ordered a .38 caliber revolver and a World War II-era Italian rifle with a telescopic sight.

Living nearby in Dallas at this time was the outspoken, ultra-rightwing, militantly anticommunist retired Major General Edwin Walker, who was in the midst of a speaking tour condemning the Civil Rights Movement and the Kennedy administration, and calling for a full invasion of Cuba to rout the communists.

During March of 1963, Oswald carefully documented a plan to assassinate Walker. Standing in their backyard, he had Marina take photos of him posed with his guns, holding up copies of socialist newspapers, *The Worker* and *The Militant*. He inscribed one photo "To Junie" saying it was "to remember Papa by sometimes."

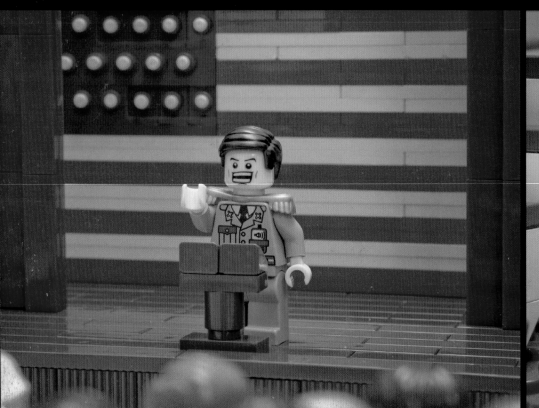

Oswald had also just completed writing a rambling political manifesto, in which he predicted that a "total crisis" would soon destroy the US government and that a small elite party would pick up the pieces to establish a "democratic, pure communist society" that would include free speech, racial and religious tolerance, abolition of all armies, and gun control.

On April 10, Oswald left behind a note for his wife in case of his death or capture, and after eating dinner at home, traveled to the woods outside Walker's house where, in previous preparations, he had buried his rifle.

From a distance of about 100 feet, Oswald found a clear shot through a window at General Walker, who was seated at his desk, doing his taxes. Suddenly, the window glass shattered, and a bullet whizzed past Walker's head, missing by inches.

Oswald quickly reburied the rifle, not knowing whether he'd hit or missed Walker. Lacking a driver's license or car, Oswald had timed the shooting to coincide with the end of a Mormon church service nearby. Making his way to the local bus stop, he was unnoticed amid the parishioners and made his escape.

Though he laughed at the Dallas police's inability to solve the Walker shooting, at Marina's insistence, he left town, traveling to New Orleans where he lived mostly on unemployment checks and began handing out pro-Castro leaflets downtown, urging the US government to stay out of Cuba's affairs.

After twice being arrested for public scuffles with anti-Castro Cuban political exiles, in August Oswald was invited to appear on two radio programs where, in a sophisticated manner, he discussed and debated his objections to President Kennedy's Cuban policy.

Now determined to defect to Cuba, in late September Oswald gathered evidence of his pro-Castro activities in New Orleans and brought them to the Cuban Consulate in Mexico City, expecting to be welcomed as a fellow revolutionary Marxist.

Wary of him, the consulate was unwilling to issue him a visa. Outraged, Oswald angrily demanded better treatment for all he had done for the Cuban cause. Consul Eusebio Azcue became offended and told Oswald that the revolution did not need friends like him, telling him to leave or be thrown out.

Dejected, Oswald returned to Texas and reunited with his nine-month pregnant wife and baby daughter. Needing funds to support them, Oswald took another menial job offered through a friend, this time working at the Texas School Book Depository in Dallas.

The FBI, which had periodically checked up on Oswald since his return from the USSR, wanted to speak to Oswald again after learning of his trip to the Cuban Consulate in Mexico City. In early November, agent James Hosty spoke briefly to Marina while Oswald was at work.

Believing that the FBI's intrusions into his life had already cost him previous jobs, Oswald wrote a threatening letter to the FBI. On a lunch break from his job at the book depository, Oswald walked to the nearby Dallas FBI headquarters, left the note with Hosty's secretary, and stormed out.

By mid-November, Dallas newspapers were abuzz with reports about President Kennedy's upcoming visit, and on the 19th, the specific route of the motorcade was given, passing directly in front of the book depository.

The morning of Kennedy's arrival, Oswald kissed his newborn daughter Audrey and twenty-month-old June goodbye. He left all the money he had, $170, on a dresser, telling Marina to buy whatever she and the children needed. He also secretly left his wedding ring in a teacup.

He then drove to work with a coworker, carrying a package wrapped in brown paper that he said contained curtain rods. By 8 AM, Oswald was at work, fulfilling orders as usual, including the retrieval of books from boxes stored on the sixth floor.

At 12:30 PM, Kennedy's motorcade, en route from the airport to a business luncheon at the Dallas Trade Mart, turned right onto Houston Street, heading toward the book depository. In the limousine with the president and First Lady Jacqueline Kennedy were Texas Governor John Connally and

In the southeast corner of the sixth floor, Oswald
stacked boxes so that he would not be noticed.
Then, he took the same rifle he'd fired at General
Walker seven months before and positioned himself at the open window with a perfect view of the
motorcade.

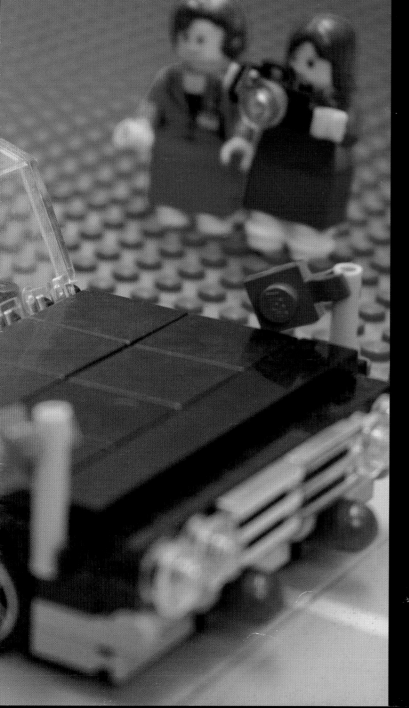

The president's limousine turned left onto Elm Street just in front of the depository. Among the crowds lining the streets, a few noticed a man with a rifle perched in the window of the book depository but assumed he was there to protect the president. Amid the cheers of the crowd, a loud bang sounded.

No one was hit, but hearing the shot, Governor Connally turned to his right. Within three seconds, another shot was fired, and this one hit Kennedy at the base of his neck, passed through him, and hit Connally in the back. "My God!" the governor said. "They're going to kill us all!"

Realizing something was wrong, Jacqueline Kennedy turned toward her husband, but seconds later a third shot hit the president in the back of the head, exploding blood, brain matter, and skull fragments all over the limousine.

"They've killed my husband," the first lady was heard to say. "I have his brains in my hand." She then climbed out of her seat and onto the trunk of the limousine. Meanwhile, Secret Service Agent Clint Hill climbed onto the back of the car to protect the first lady. "My God," she cried, "they have shot his head off."

Acting on tips that shots came from the book depository, police officer Marrion Baker quickly began searching the building with depository supervisor Roy Truly. In the second floor lunchroom, they came across Oswald holding a bottle of Coca-Cola. Baker asked Truly if Oswald was an employee, Truly said yes, and they moved on.

Three minutes after the shooting, Oswald exited the depository by the front door, just before police sealed off the building. The rifle left behind on the sixth floor was quickly found, and soon a description of the man spotted in the window during the shooting was broadcast to all area police.

Just over an hour after the shooting, Dallas police officer J. D. Tippit spotted Oswald walking through a neighborhood three miles from where the president was shot. He exchanged some words with him through the window of his patrol car.

As Tippit got out of his car and approached Oswald with his gun still holstered, Oswald drew his revolver and shot Tippit three times in the chest. Tippit collapsed, then Oswald shot him a final time in the head.

There were several witnesses to Tippit's murder, one of whom believed he heard Oswald mutter, "Poor, dumb cop," as he fled the scene while reloading his gun. Another witness used the patrol car's radio to call for help.

A few blocks away, Oswald ducked into a movie theater without buying a ticket. Spotted by a shoe salesman across the street from the theater, the police were notified of the man's description and soon surrounded the theater.

Oswald was captured at 1:45 PM, sitting by himself during a showing of the movie, *War Is Hell*. "Well, it's all over now," he said, before trying to punch a policeman and draw his revolver. He was quickly overpowered and beaten down.

Interrogated for hours at police headquarters, Oswald repeatedly denied shooting Tippit or President Kennedy. Confronted with his Mannlicher-Carcano rifle, he denied owning any rifles. Affirming he was a Marxist, he said he had no reason to kill Kennedy, as he would be replaced by someone who would continue his policies.

At midnight, Oswald was paraded in front of the press gathered at the police station. "They've taken me in because of the fact that I lived in the Soviet Union," Oswald told reporters. "I'm just a patsy." Posing as a member of the press that night was a local strip club owner named Jacob Rubenstein, better known as Jack Ruby.

Distraught over the president's assassination, Ruby hung around police headquarters all weekend, carrying his .38 caliber revolver in his pocket. On Saturday, he had no chance to get close to Oswald as he was shuttled back and forth between interrogations and police lineups.

But on Sunday morning, as Oswald was being lead out of the basement garage of the police headquarters before live TV cameras, the fifty-two-year-old Ruby stepped out of the crowd and shot Oswald in the chest, shouting, "You killed my president, you rat!"

The twenty-four-year-old Oswald was soon pronounced dead. Questioned by police about his motive, Ruby said he wanted to spare the first lady the agony of a trial, and later added, "I guess I just had to show the world that a Jew has guts."

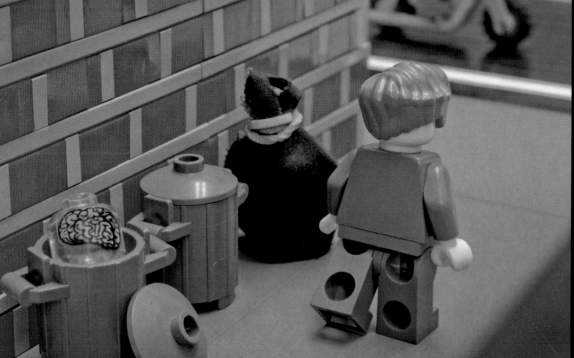

After President Kennedy's autopsy, his brain, several tissue samples, and blood slides were turned over to the Kennedy family. In 1966, they were discovered to be missing. It is likely that they were disposed of by Robert Kennedy, so it would not come out that his brother had Addison's disease and had been taking steroids to treat it.

RICHARD NIXON
February 22, 1974

Samuel Joseph Byck was born in 1930, to a poor Jewish family in Philadelphia. He dropped out of high school and worked various short-term jobs before joining the army at age twenty-four. During his two-year stint, he received training in firearms and explosives.

Byck married in 1957, and had four children. But his inability to hold a steady job and his failed business ventures put a strain on his marriage. In late 1968, Byck applied to the Small Business Administration (SBA) for a $20,000 loan to start a business selling tires out of a brightly painted remodeled school bus.

Then, in 1969, Byck committed himself to a psychiatric hospital for a month of inpatient treatment for anxiety and depression. While there, he received notice that his loan from the SBA had been denied. He was diagnosed with manic-depressive illness.

Rather than see mental illness as the root of his problems, Byck became convinced that, like millions of other poor Americans, he was the victim of a hopelessly corrupt political system. In 1972, Byck expressed his admiration for those willing to take a stand against societal injustice by contributing $500 and some tires to the Black Panthers.

Later that same year, he was questioned by the Secret Service after he was reported commenting that someone ought to kill President Nixon. Byck denied making such a statement, and a psychiatrist who had treated him told investigators that Byck was a "big talker who makes verbal threats and never acts on them."

By early 1973, now estranged from his wife and children, Byck began thinking of ways to end his life in a symbolic and violent way. He found inspiration in a newspaper article about a man who also hated Nixon and who had lashed out at society by shooting six people from the top of a Howard Johnson's hotel in New Orleans.

Over the next year, Byck made trips to Washington, DC, where he was arrested for picketing in front of the White House without a permit. On two additional occasions, he was questioned by the Secret Service, but not arrested. On Christmas Eve of 1973, he donned a Santa suit and stood in front of the White House with an "Impeach Nixon" sign.

In early 1974, the forty-four-year-old Byck read up on past assassins and made a series of rambling tape recordings in which he laid out his grievances about his family and personal life, vented his anger at the corrupt SBA and their denial of his loan, and expressed many condemnations of the Nixon administration.

He also matter of factly described his plans for what he called "Operation Pandora's Box," in which he planned to hijack an airliner, force the pilots to fly it low over Washington, DC, then shoot the pilots dead and crash the plane into the White House, killing Nixon and as many of his Watergate cohorts as possible.

Wanting to ensure his motives were understood, and hoping to avoid being dismissed as some mere lunatic assassin, Byck sent copies of his tape recordings to people he admired, including scientist Jonas Salk, composer Leonard Bernstein, Senator Abraham Ribicoff of Connecticut, and newspaper columnist Jack Anderson.

In the early morning hours of February 22, 1974, Byck drove from Philadelphia to the Baltimore/Washington International Airport. He was armed with a homemade suitcase gasoline bomb and a .22 caliber pistol he stole from a friend. As he drove, he made final recordings in which he noted that "one man's terrorist is another man's patriot."

Byck entered the airport at 7 AM and walked to the gate of a plane that was just starting to board for a 7:15 AM departure to Atlanta. Approaching airport police officer Neal Ramsburg, Byck shot him twice in the back, instantly killing him. He then jumped over a security chain and ran down the boarding ramp onto the plane.

Pilot Reese Lofton was going through a preflight checklist, and copilot Freddie Jones was cleaning his pipe, when a panting, sweating Byck stormed into the cockpit. "I've got this bomb," he announced. He demanded the plane take off, and then shot copilot Jones in the head, mortally wounding him.

Airport police officer Charles Troyer was at an airport coffee shop when he heard gunfire. Running toward the panicked scene at the gate, he found officer Ramsburg lying in a pool of blood. Determining he was dead, he took Ramsburg's holstered .357 Magnum revolver and headed for the plane.

Pilot Lofton started the engines but informed Byck that the plane's door would have to be closed for takeoff. Byck shouted at the crew for the door to be closed. Two flight attendants then exited the plane to close the door from the outside.

Running down the boarding ramp, Officer Troyer spotted a man facing the cockpit and holding a gun. He shouted for the flight attendants to flee and then fired his weapon as the door swung shut, his bullets ricocheting off the edge of the door.

Panicked, Byck fired into the cockpit, hitting both pilots in the back and shoulder areas.

Taking the stairs down to the tarmac, Troyer joined other officers who were attempting to shoot out the tires of the plane. But the bullets failed to penetrate the thick rubber and ricocheted, at least one hitting the plane's wing.

From the eight passengers who had boarded the plane before him, Byck grabbed a woman out of her first-class seat, dragged her to the cockpit, and told her, "Help this man fly this plane."

Lofton spent six weeks in the hospital but recovered from his wounds and returned to piloting. President Nixon was in the White House at the time of the hijacking, attempting to limit the damage of the Watergate scandal that would cause him to resign the presidency months later to avoid impeachment.

Chapter 11
GERALD FORD
September 5, 1975

As a child in the 1950s, Lynette Fromme was part of a Los Angeles dance troupe that toured the United States, appeared on TV's *The Lawrence Welk Show*, and even performed at the White House for President Dwight Eisenhower.

Fromme grew rebellious in her teenage years, got into fights with her father, and experimented with drugs and alcohol. Eventually, her disciplinarian father kicked her out of the house during her first year at junior college.

Freshly released from a stint in prison, thirty-two-year-old Charles Manson came across a depressed Fromme staring at the ocean at Venice Beach. He immediately charmed her, and Fromme joined a growing number of female followers who treated Manson as a religious guru, lover, and father figure.

In the summer of 1968, the Manson Family, as it came to be known, took up residence with Dennis Wilson of the Beach Boys and convinced record industry executives to fund a recording session of Manson's songs, backed up by the Family.

By late 1968, the Family set themselves up on an old movie ranch owned by eighty-year-old George Spahn. At Manson's direction, Fromme engaged in a sexual relationship with Spahn, and the Family was allowed to stay there rent free.

Hoping to spark an apocalyptic, genocidal race war, in August of 1969, Manson ordered his followers to carry out the gruesome Tate/LaBianca murder spree, attempting to leave behind false evidence that the murders were committed by African Americans.

Fromme had not participated in the murders, but when Manson and others were arrested and brought to trial, she joined fellow Family members who shaved their heads, carved x's on their foreheads, and held constant vigil outside the courthouse.

Once Manson had been sent to prison for life, Fromme and another Family member moved to Sacramento and began wearing red-robed outfits, considering themselves nuns awaiting the release of their Lord. In the early '70s, Fromme dedicated herself to combating one of the evils that Manson had warned about: industrial polluters.

Forming what she called the International People's Court of Retribution, Fromme made plans for Manson followers to carry out grisly murders of the CEOs of major polluters and their wives. She wrote letters and made phone calls urging others to action but soon realized such plans could not succeed without Manson to lead them.

Fromme was desperate for a way to get Manson back into a courtroom to explain himself to the world when she found out that President Gerald Ford would be visiting Sacramento. On the morning of September 5, 1975, Ford left the Senator Hotel to walk the short distance to the state capitol.

From amid the crowd gathered to see the president, twenty-six-year-old Fromme pulled out a borrowed .45 caliber semiautomatic pistol she had strapped to her leg under her robes and aimed it directly at the president's crotch.

"It didn't go off!" shouted Fromme repeatedly as she was wrestled to the ground by Secret Service members. It is unknown whether Fromme intended to shoot Ford. The pistol was later found to be loaded, but there was no bullet in the chamber.

When the judge denied her request to represent herself and call her own witnesses, Fromme completely refused to participate in her own trial, at one point telling the judge, "Your Honor, I feel all the laws were broken when Manson was put in prison."

After a lengthy trial, Fromme was convicted of attempted assassination. When US Attorney Dwayne Keyes recommended severe punishment because she was "full of hate and violence," Fromme removed an apple from under her robe and threw it at him, hitting him in the face and knocking off his glasses.

While in prison in 1979, Fromme injured a fellow inmate when she struck her in the head with the claw end of a hammer as the two were tending a garden on the prison grounds.

In December of 1987, Fromme managed to escape from prison after hearing that Manson was dying of testicular cancer. The rumor turned out to be false, and Fromme was caught two days later just two miles from the prison.

Having served thirty-four years behind bars, Fromme was released on parole in 2009 at age sixty and took up residence in Oneida County, New York, where to date she has had no further run-ins with the law.

Chapter 12
GERALD FORD
September 22, 1975

Seventeen days after Lynette Fromme pointed a gun at him from two feet away, President Ford was in San Francisco, making his way out of the St. Francis Hotel at 3:30 PM, surrounded by heavy security.

Standing on the other side of the street, forty-five-year-old Sara Jane Moore had been waiting amid a crowd for three hours, hoping to get a glimpse of the president. When he appeared, Moore took her .38 caliber revolver from her purse, aimed it at the president's head, and fired.

By pure coincidence, Moore also had a connection to Charles Manson. As children, Moore and Manson both grew up in Charlotte, West Virginia, and bought candy from the same grocery store where Manson's mother was briefly employed.

As a child, young "Sally," as she liked to be called, was a straight-A student, studied ballet, was an excellent seamstress, and played violin. Her comfortable middle-class family would often gather to play their instruments together.

Wanting to escape her overly strict Baptist father, Moore left home after high school. Impulsively she married a marine for a month, and within a week of annulling that marriage, she married an air force officer with whom she had three children before filing for divorce.

In 1958, Moore moved to Los Angeles and married a minor movie executive, eventually leaving her three children behind to be raised by their grandparents in West Virginia.

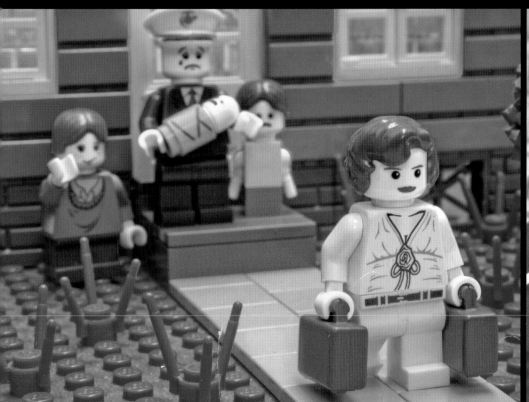

Moore had a fourth child but soon separated from the boy's father. She took her son to the San Francisco Bay Area where she trained to become a certified professional accountant and married a fourth husband, a wealthy physician.

But this marriage soon also soured and was annulled. In 1974, Moore became obsessed with the news stories of the Symbionese Liberation Army's (SLA) kidnapping and brainwashing of Patty Hearst, the daughter of newspaper publisher Randolph Hearst.

When the SLA demanded a ransom of $2 million in food to be given to the poor, Randolph Hearst established the People in Need fund, and Moore volunteered her accounting skills. Noting her dedication, Hearst asked Moore if she might develop contacts among the radical left in San Francisco to help find his daughter.

Living in San Francisco's Mission District, Moore immersed herself in revolutionary left-wing political writings and cultivated friendships with people like United Prisoners Union Head Wilbert "Popeye" Jackson at parties and counter-culture events.

Taking note of her new acquaintances, the FBI approached Moore in the spring of 1974, asking her to become an informant for the radical movements they hoped to keep a tight watch on in those turbulent times. Flattered by the attention and the importance of her role, Moore agreed.

The more time Moore spent among the radicals, though, the more she sympathized with their revolutionary ideology, and the more she felt accepted by them. Feeling she was betraying her friends, she decided to stop informing on them and come clean with them about it.

Consequently shunned by her radical friends and useless to the FBI, Moore didn't know what to do next. Then, on June 8, 1975, "Popeye" Jackson and his girlfriend were shot to death as they sat in a car in Moore's neighborhood. An anonymous caller told Moore, "You're next."

Moore decided to buy herself a .44 caliber revolver and made trips to the shooting range for practice. She brought her son with her to live in an apartment in the East Bay suburbs for most of July but returned to San Francisco by August.

On September 5, Moore learned of Lynette Fromme's attempt on President Ford's life. On the 18th, Patty Hearst and another SLA member were captured by police. Terrified that she would be blamed for their arrest, Moore called the police and threatened the president, hoping they would take her into custody where she would be safe.

The police visited Moore and confiscated her .44 caliber revolver. Secret Service agents also interviewed her but decided she was not enough of a threat to warrant surveillance during the president's visit to San Francisco.

The next morning, Moore dropped her son off at school and drove out to the East Bay suburbs to buy a new gun, this time a .38 caliber revolver. She loaded it while driving back across the Bay Bridge into San Francisco.

Feeling desperate and hoping to do something that would prove herself to the radical friends she had betrayed, Moore went to Union Square to join the throngs of others waiting to see the president as he emerged from his hotel.

Moore's first shot missed the president's head by about six inches, likely because she hadn't adjusted the sights on her new gun. She was about to line up a second shot when a decorated ex-marine named Oliver Sipple shouted, "Gun!" and grabbed her arm, pulling her down.

Immediately after the shooting, Moore was dragged into the St. Francis Hotel, where she was questioned by police. She explained that she knew she'd fired too high and noted, "If I had had my .44 with me, I would have caught him."

Sipple was immediately hailed by the press as a hero, but he did not want the media attention. He had not revealed to his family that he was gay and worried that now, since he was a well-known member of San Francisco's gay community, such news would be leaked.

Indeed, newspapers soon hailed the "Homosexual Hero" who saved the president's life. Sipple's family back in Detroit was mortified. His father and two brothers endured taunting and laughter at the GM factory where they worked. Sipple's mother stopped talking to him for years.

Sipple received a letter of thanks from President Ford but was never invited to the White House. As years went by, Sipple became a heavy drinker and sometimes told people he wished he had never acted to save Ford's life. He died at age forty-seven in 1989.

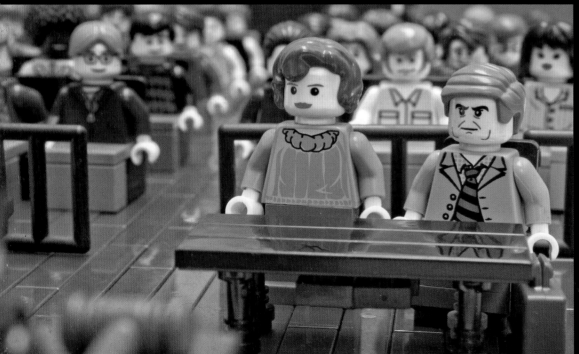

After being examined by psychologists, Moore was found fit to stand trial. She pled guilty and made a statement before the court, affirming that she had known what she was doing, and then added, "To those of you who share my dream of a new revolution in this land of ours, I say, 'Fight on.'"

Moore was sentenced to life in prison. In 1979, she and a fellow inmate climbed a barbed wire fence and briefly escaped. After running through the snowy Appalachian foothills and hitchhiking twenty miles, they were caught a few hours later.

Released from prison in 2008 at age seventy-seven, Moore appeared as a guest on NBC's *The Today Show*, saying, "We were saying the country needed to change. The only way it was going to change was a violent revolution. I genuinely thought that this might trigger that new revolution in this country."

Chapter 13
RONALD REAGAN
March 30, 1981

The youngest of three children born to a Midwest oil executive,
John Hinckley, Jr. was active in sports throughout middle school
but became increasingly reclusive in his high school years, spending most of his time alone in his room, listening to Beatles albums
and playing guitar.

In 1980, Hinckley convinced his parents to give him $3,600 to attend a writer's workshop at Yale University where Jodie Foster had just enrolled. Once there, Hinckley left the celebrity freshman love notes under her door, followed her from a distance around campus, and twice managed to speak to her on the phone but was politely told to leave her alone.

Hinckley then decided he would have to do something dramatic to get Foster to take his love for her seriously. For two weeks in October, Hinckley stalked President Jimmy Carter across the United States, flying from city to city. At the Nashville Airport, police arrested Hinckley and confiscated three handguns he was carrying in his suitcase, just hours before the president landed.

After paying a fine, Hinckley was released. He then flew to Dallas and purchased two new handguns while visiting his sister. Then he flew to Washington, DC, still looking for an opportunity to assassinate Carter. As the election approached, however, polls showed that Carter would soon be defeated, and Hinckley lost interest.

As he usually did when he ran out of money, Hinckley returned to his parents' house in Colorado. At their insistence, he began to see a psychiatrist. In his many therapy sessions over the coming months, Hinckley never mentioned his obsession with Jodie Foster or the violent crimes he was considering carrying out.

In December of 1980, Hinckley began stalking President-elect Reagan, but was interrupted on the 8th, when his hero John Lennon was assassinated in New York City. Immediately getting on a plane, Hinckley joined the great mass of mourners gathered in Central Park.

While in New York, Hinckley sought out the services of underage prostitutes. He soon became fascinated by Lennon's assassin, the similarly chubby social outcast Mark David Chapman. Returning to Colorado in January, he went to a sporting goods store and purchased the same model handgun that was used to kill Lennon.

During this time, Hinckley wrote poems such as "Guns are Fun!": See that living legend over there? / With one little squeeze of this trigger / I can put that person at my feet / moaning and groaning and pleading with God / This gun gives me pornographic power / If I wish, the president will fall / and the world will look at me in disbelief / all because I own an inexpensive gun / Guns are lovable, Guns are fun / Are you lucky enough to own one?

With Lennon's death, Hinckley now felt he had only Jodie Foster to live for. When his father finally put his foot down in early March 1981, and refused to continue financially supporting his wayward twenty-five-year-old son, Hinckley took a bus to Washington, DC. On March 30, while eating breakfast at McDonald's and reading a newspaper, he noticed the newly inaugurated president's daily schedule.

Returning to his hotel room, Hinckley wrote a final letter to Foster, in which he acknowledged that he might be killed while trying to assassinate Reagan, but that he could not wait any longer to do something to impress her. He then sorted through his ammunition and loaded six Devastator hollow point bullets into his .22 caliber revolver, tucked it into his jacket pocket, went outside, and hailed a cab.

Hinckley saw President Reagan enter the Hilton Hotel at 1:45 PM, and bided his time in the lobby while the president made his speech to AFL-CIO leaders. Then, jostling for a position with TV crews just outside the side entrance, Hinckley staked out a spot by the security rope.

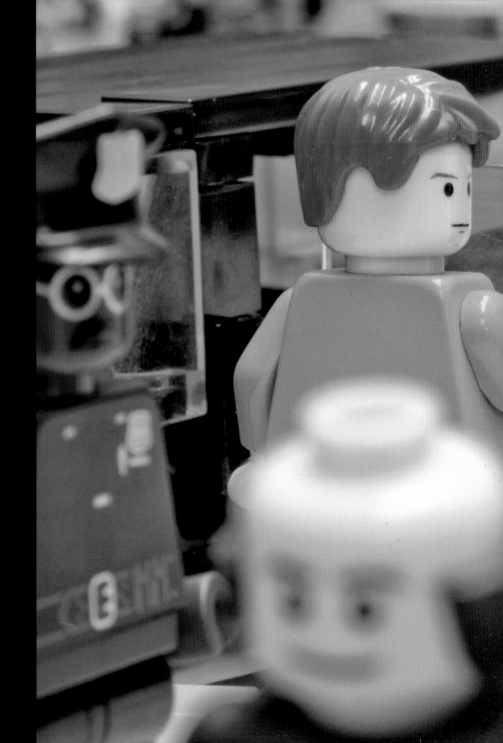

Reagan and his entourage emerged from the Hilton at 2:25 PM. The smiling president waved toward onlookers across the street as he headed for his waiting limousine about twenty feet away, then turned to wave toward the press on his left.

With about fifteen feet separating him from the president, Hinckley took his revolver out of his pocket, steadied the gun with both hands, and fired six times in two seconds, tracking his target's movement from right to left.

At the sound of gunfire, Secret Service Agent Jerry Parr forced the president down behind the limousine's door just in time for its bulletproof glass to stop a bullet from hitting the president's head. While moving to shield the president, Agent Tim McCarthy took a bullet in the stomach. Washington, DC, police officer Tom Delahanty was struck in the neck, and Press Secretary James Brady collapsed after being shot in the head.

A senior citizen standing behind Hinckley slammed his arms down on the assassin's neck, shouting, "Kill the son of a bitch!" In seconds, numerous police officers and Secret Service agents had piled on top of the shooter as McCarthy, Delahanty, and Brady lay on the sidewalk, bleeding from their wounds.

Pushed hard into the backseat of the limousine, Reagan felt a pain in his side, as if someone had hit him with a hammer. Thinking it was the result of agent Parr's rough handling of him, the seventy-year-old president half-jokingly scolded him, "You son of a bitch, you broke my rib!"

But when Parr noticed the corner of Reagan's mouth frothy with blood, he knew something was very wrong. He ordered the limousine to drive to George Washington University Hospital. Arriving ten minutes later, the president was not put on a stretcher but rather walked inside with Parr's help before collapsing inside the door, saying, "I can't breathe."

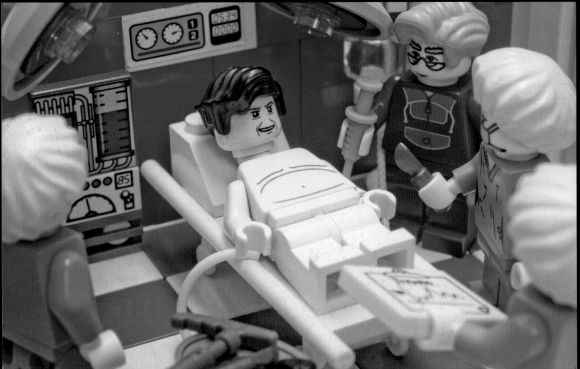

Doctors discovered an entry wound just below the president's left armpit. Reagan had been hit by Hinckley's sixth and final bullet, which flattened as it ricocheted off the side of the limousine and lodged an inch from his heart. Just before being put under for surgery, the president said to his team of surgeons, "Please, tell me you're Republicans."

Though not completely recovered until some six months later, Reagan returned to the White House just twelve days after the shooting. Erring on the side of caution that day, under his sweater he wore a bulletproof vest. Reagan had become the first sitting president to survive being shot by an assassin.

During Hinckley's trial, Jodie Foster was subpoenaed to testify. At a videotaped session that was later shown to the jury, she calmly answered lawyers' questions about being stalked. When asked to describe her relationship with John Hinckley, she stated, "I have no relationship with John Hinckley." At this, Hinckley threw a pen at her and screamed, "I'll get you, Foster!" as he was restrained by marshals.

gal team defending his son, and they summoned a team of psychologists to argue their case that Hinckley was not guilty by reason of insanity. The defense concluded with an airing of the movie *Taxi Driver* for the jury in its entirety.

acquitted of all charges. He was then committed to St. Elizabeths Hospital in Washington, DC, where he described a typical day as including playing his guitar, shooting pool, and listening to music. Looking back, he described the Reagan shooting as "the greatest love offering in the history of the world," and noted, "God does indeed work in mysterious ways."

Officer Delahanty recovered from his neck wound but suffered permanent nerve damage. In 1986, he sued the manufacturer of the gun used by Hinckley, hoping to spur the court into imposing a ban on all small, cheap handguns of the type favored by criminals. The court rejected his case.

In 1987, Hinckley's requests for more privileges at St. Elizabeths were denied when it was discovered that he had exchanged letters with serial killer Ted Bundy. After receiving a letter from would-be Gerald Ford assassin Lynette Fromme, Hinckley had also sought a mailing address for Charles Manson. In addition, a cache of photo clippings of Jodie Foster was found in his room.

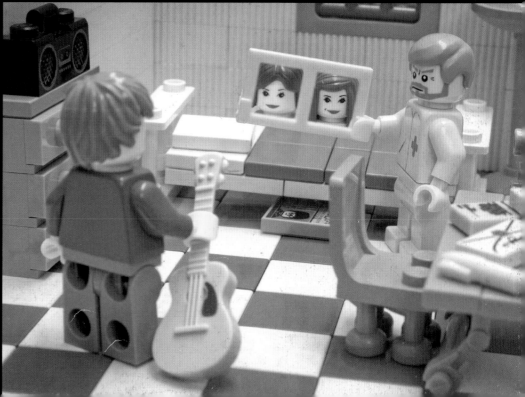

James Brady's wounds left him with partial paralysis and slurred speech. He became a strong advocate of handgun control and assault weapon restrictions. In 1993, despite a massive lobbying campaign by the NRA, Congress passed and President Bill Clinton signed the Brady Bill, instituting mandatory background checks on most gun sales.

Over the past two decades, Hinckley has been allowed unsupervised visits of various lengths to see his mother at her home in Virginia. He has dated multiple women, and in 2009, he recorded "Ballad of an Outlaw," a song he wrote before the Reagan shooting. Its lyrics have been described as "reflecting suicide and lawlessness."

Chapter 14

BILL CLINTON
November 1996

In late November 1996, the recently reelected President Bill
Clinton was in the Philippines attending an economic summit.

Finding himself late for a meeting with a senior member of the Philippine government, Clinton instructed his motorcade to get him to his meeting in a hurry.

But while en route, a Secret Service agent received a crackly message through his earpiece: intelligence operators had intercepted and partially decoded a radio transmission referencing a bridge and an assassination. Despite Clinton's strenuous protest, the motorcade was rerouted.

A US intelligence team was sent to investigate and discovered an extremely powerful bomb had been placed underneath a bridge in a busy area of downtown Manila.

Further investigation of this plot to assassinate President Clinton revealed that it had been masterminded by a Saudi terrorist living in Afghanistan named Osama bin Laden.

Chapter 15

BARACK OBAMA
November 11, 2011

Born in 1990, Oscar Ramiro Ortega-Hernandez grew up in
Idaho Falls, Idaho, where he dropped out of school in tenth grade.
He then worked as a waiter in his family's Mexican restaurant

Ortega often partied with his friends on weekends and had a number of minor run-ins with the law, including indictments for drug offenses and underage drinking.

In 2010, at age twenty, Ortega grew out his hair and beard and began a year of intensive training to become a mixed martial arts fighter. In his first and only bout, he pummeled his opponent in the face until the referee ruled it a technical knockout.

Standing in triumph, Ortega held his infant son, whom he had named Israel.

In March of 2011, Ortega purchased an assault rifle from twenty-one-year-old Jake Chapman, known to friends as "the gun guy." Chapman recalled that about a year earlier, Ortega had watched an antigovernment Internet movie called, *The Obama Deception*.

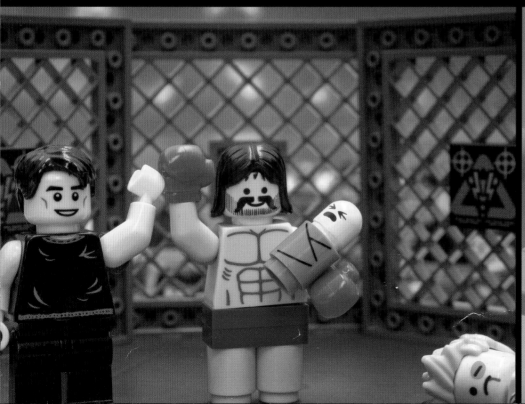

In September, Ortega convinced a student from Idaho State University to help him shoot a video intended for Oprah Winfrey, begging her to bring him on her TV talk show as a guest. "I have been sent here from God," claims Ortega in the video. "I also have with me the answer to worldwide peace."

In a disjointed twenty-minute talk, Ortega said he had received a "message through time" while watching a History Channel show about Nostradamus. He ended by noting, "It's not just a coincidence that I look like Jesus. I am the modern-day Jesus that you all have been waiting for."

At his twenty-first birthday party in October, surrounded by family, Ortega gave a forty-five-minute speech in support of marijuana legalization, condemning the government's bullying of foreign oil-producing countries, and detailing the threat of secret societies.

Talking with friends, Ortega expressed a belief that President Barack Obama planned to implant GPS tracking devices in children. He also referred to the president variously as "the Antichrist" and "the Devil," and said he "needed to kill him" and that he would "not stop until it's done."

Telling his family he was heading on a vacation to Utah, Ortega instead drove across the country. On November 11, 2011, just outside Washington, DC, Ortega was reported as acting suspiciously. On foot and unarmed, he was briefly questioned by police who took his photo, but he was allowed to go.

Later that evening, at about 9 PM, Ortega allegedly drove into Washington and stopped his car on Constitution Avenue, about 700 yards from the White House. Aiming through a telescopic sight, he allegedly pointed his assault rifle out the passenger side window.

Authorities believe nine rounds were fired. Several hit the walls of the first family's living quarters, and at least one bullet flew across a balcony, often used by the Obamas to relax, and broke the outer window, but it was stopped by an inner layer of ballistic glass.

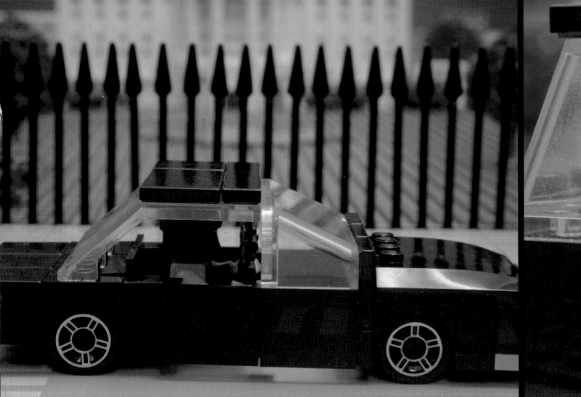

Witnesses saw Ortega speed on, but only a few blocks away his car came to a stop on the lawn of the US Institute of Peace. After briefly trying to restart the car, he was seen abandoning it and fleeing the scene on foot.

When investigators searched the car, they found the assault rifle, three clips of ammunition, brass knuckles, an aluminum baseball bat, and the hooded jacket in which police had photographed Ortega earlier that day.

A photo of the suspect was issued to law enforcement, and five days later Ortega was arrested without incident in the lobby of a hotel in western Pennsylvania. He was charged with attempted assassination, and his trial was scheduled for fall 2013.

The president and First Lady Michelle Obama
were en route to Hawaii at the time of the shooting.
The Secret Service has not commented on whether
the Obamas' daughters, Sasha and Malia, were at the
White House during the incident.

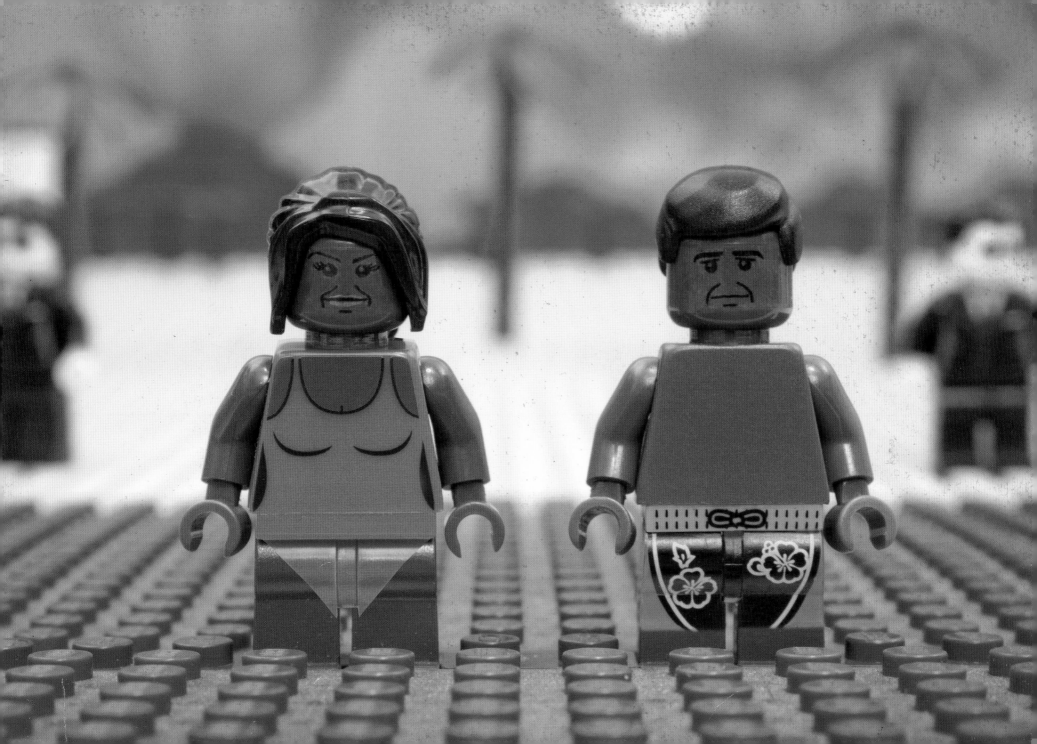

THE END

BIBLIOGRAPHY

Chapter 1

Brands, H. W. *Andrew Jackson: His Life and Times.* New York: Anchor, 2006.

Burnstein, Andrew. *The Passions of Andrew Jackson.* New York: Vintage, 2004.

Clarke, James W. *American Assassins.* Princeton: Princeton University Press, 1982.

Freeman, Katie. "Letter threatening Jackson's life determined to be written by father of man who killed Lincoln" *Knoxnews.com*, 2009. www.knoxnews.com/news/2009/jan/25/letter-threatening-jacksons-life-determined-writte/ (accessed December 14, 2012).

Mintz, S. and S. McNeil. "Political Assassination: The Violent Side of American Political Life." *Digitalhistory.uh.edu*, 2003. www.digitalhistory.uh.edu/topic_display.cfm?tcid=98 (accessed December 14, 2012).

Remin, Robert V. *The Life of Andrew Jackson.* New York: Harper Perennial, 1999.

Spignesi, Stephen J. *In the Crosshairs: Famous Assassinations & Attempts From Julius Caesar to John Lennon.* Darby, PA: Diane Publishing Co., 2003.

Chapters 2 and 3

Axelrod, Alan. *The Complete Idiot's Guide to the Civil War, 3rd Edition.* New York: ALPHA, 2011.

Clarke, Asia. *John Wilkes Booth: A Sister's Memoir.* Jackson: University Press of Mississippi, 1999.

Clarke, James W. *American Assassins*. Princeton: Princeton University Press, 1982.

Donald, David Herbert. *Lincoln*. New York: Simon & Schuster, 1996.

Goodwin, Doris Kearns. *Team of Rivals: The Political Genius of Abraham Lincoln*. New York: Simon & Schuster, 2005.

Hartranft, John Frederick. *The Lincoln Assassination Conspirators: Their Confinement and Execution, As Recorded in the Letterbook of John Frederick Hartranft*. Baton Rouge: LSU Press, 2009.

Hatch, Frederick. *Protecting President Lincoln: The Security Effort, the Thwarted Plots and the Disaster at Ford's Theatre*. Jefferson, NC: McFarland, 2011.

Kauffman, Michael W. *American Brutus*. New York: Random Hous, 2005.

Kimmel, Stanley. *The Mad Booths of Maryland*. Mineola, NY: Dover, 1970.

Smith, Gene. *American Gothic: The Story of America's Legendary Theatrical Family—Junius, Edwin, and John Wilkes Booth*. New York: Simon & Schuster, 1992.

Spignesi, Stephen J. *In the Crosshairs: Famous Assassinations & Attempts From Julius Caesar to John Lennon*. Darby, PA: Diane Publishing Co., 2003.

Steers Jr, Edward. *Blood on the Moon: The Assassination of Abraham Lincoln*. Louisville: The University Press of Kentucky, 2005.

Swanson, James L. *Manhunt*. New York: William Morrow, 2007.

Swanson, James L. and Daniel Weinberg. *Lincoln's Assassins: Their Trial and Execution*. New York: Harper Perennial, 2008.

Wilson, Western W. *"Abe" Lincoln's Yarns and Stories*. Chicago: The Educational Company, 1901.

Chapter 4

Bliss, D. W. "The Story of President Garfield's Illness," *Century Magazine*, no. 1 (1881).

Clarke, James W. *American Assassins*. Princeton: Princeton University Press, 1982.

Hayes, C. J., Annie J. Dunmire, and Edmund A. Bailey. *A complete history of the life and trial of Charles Julius Guiteau, assassin of President Garfield*. Philadelphia: Hubbard Bros., 1882.

Millard, Candice. *Destiny of the Republic: A Tale of Madness, Medicine and the Murder of a President*. New York: Anchor, 2012.

Rosenberg, Charles E. *The Trial of the Assassin Guiteau: Psychiatry and the Law in the Gilded Age*. Chicago: University of Chicago Press, 1995.

Spignesi, Stephen J. *In the Crosshairs: Famous Assassinations & Attempts From Julius Caesar to John Lennon*. Darby, PA: Diane Publishing Co., 2003.

Chapter 5

Clarke, James W. *American Assassins*. Princeton: Princeton University Press, 1982.

Leech, Margaret. *In the Days of McKinley*. Newtown, CT: American Political Biography Press, 1999.

Miller, Scott. *The President and the Assassin*. New York: Random House, 2011.

Peterson, Harold F. "Buffalo Builds the 1901 Pan-American Exposition." *Buffaloah.com*, 2008. http://buffaloah.com/h/panam/peter.html (accessed January 2, 2013).

Peterson, Merrill D. *Lincoln in American Memory*. New York: Oxford University Press, 1995.

Spignesi, Stephen J. *In the Crosshairs: Famous Assassinations & Attempts From Julius Caesar to John Lennon*. Darby, PA: Diane Publishing Co., 2003.

Vowell, Sarah. *Assassination Vacation*. New York: Simon & Schuster, 2005.

Wilson, Antoine. The Assassination of William McKinley. New York: The Rosen Publishing Group, Inc., 2002.

Zinn, Howard. *A People's History of the United States: 1492–Present*. New York: Harper, 2003.

Chapter 6

Clarke, James W. *American Assassins*. Princeton: Princeton University Press, 1982.

Cochems, Henry Frederick, and Wheeler P. Bloodgood. *The Attempted Assassination of Ex-President Theodore Roosevelt*. Milwaukee: The Progressive Publishing Company, 1912.

Donovan, Robert J. *The Assassins*. New York: Popular Library, 1964.

Millard, Candice. *The River of Doubt*. New York: Broadway Books, 2005.

Morris, Edmund. *Colonel Roosevelt*. New York: Random House, 2011.

Oehser, Paul H. "Roosevelt African Expedition Collects for Smithsonian Institute." 1970. http://siarchives.si.edu/collections/siris_sic_193 (accessed January 5, 2013).

Rauchway, Eric. *Murdering McKinley: The Making of Theodore Roosevelt's America*. New York: Hill and Wang, 2004.

Roosevelt, Theodore. "I Have Just Been Shot." 1912. http://en.wikisource.org/wiki/I_have_just_been_shot (accessed January 5, 2013).

Spignesi, Stephen J. *In the Crosshairs: Famous Assassinations & Attempts From Julius Caesar to John Lennon*. Darby, PA: Diane Publishing Co., 2003.

Denton, Sally. *The Plots Against the President: FDR, A Nation in Crisis, and the Rise of the American Right*. New York: Bloomsbury Press, 2012.

McCann, Joseph T. *Terrorism on American Soil: A Concise History of Plots and Perpetrators from the Famous to the Forgotten*. Boulder, CO: Sentient Publications, 2006.

Picci, Blaise. *The Five Weeks of Giuseppe Zangara: The Man Who Tried to Kill FDR*. Chicago: Academy Chicago Publishers, 2003.

Spignesi, Stephen J. *In the Crosshairs: Famous Assassinations & Attempts From Julius Caesar to John Lennon*. Darby, PA: Diane Publishing Co., 2003.

Chapter 7

Clarke. James W. *American Assassins*. Princeton: Princeton University Press, 1982.

Chapters 8 and 9

Blaine, Gerald, Lisa McCubbin, and Clint Hill. *The Kennedy Detail: JFK's Secret Service Agents Break Their Silence*. New York: Gallery Books, 2011.

Bugliosi, Vincent. *Four Days in November: The Assassination of President John F. Kennedy.* New York: W. W. Norton & Company, 2008.

—. *Reclaiming History: The Assassination of President John F. Kennedy.* New York: W. W. Norton & Company, 2007.

Clarke, James. W. *American Assassins.* Princeton: Princeton University Press, 1982.

David, Steve B. *Near Miss: The Attempted Assassination of JFK.* Broomfield, CO: FeedBrewer, Inc., 2010.

The Evening Independent. "'Can't Say I'd Do It Again,' 'Human Bomb' Declares." December 18, 1960. http://news.google.com/newspapers?id=LkBQAAAAIBAJ&sjid=K-FcDAAAAIBAJ&pg=4063,2642018&hl=en (accessed January 7, 2013).

Frontline. "Who Was Lee Harvey Oswald?" November 20, 2003.

John, Frederick. "Fate Foreshadowed: JFK Had Brush with Death in '60," *Deseret News.* November 19, 1989. www.deseretnews.com/article/74816/FATE-FORESHAD-OWED--JFK-HAD-BRUSH-WITH-DEATH-IN-60.html?pg=all (accessed January 7, 2013).

Kerr, Philip. "JFK: the assassin who failed." *NewStatesman,* November 27, 2000. www.newstatesman.com/node/139086 (accessed January 7, 2013).

McCann, Joseph T. *Terrorism on American Soil: A Concise History of Plots and Perpetrators from the Famous to the Forgotten.* Boulder, CO: Sentient Publications, 2006.

Oliver, Willard, and Nancy Marion. *Killing the President: Assassinations, Attempts, and Rumored Attempts on U.S. Commanders-in-Chief.* Santa Barbara: Praeger, 2010.

Posner, Gerald. *Case Closed.* New York: Anchor, 2003.

Sosin, Milt. "'Human Bomb' Held; Was After Kennedy."
The Miami News, December 16, 1960. http://news.goo-
gle.com/newspapers?nid=2206&dat=19601216&id=x-
iRmAAAAIBAJ&sjid=ReoFAAAAIBA-
J&pg=4821,138115 (accessed January 7, 2013).

Spignesi, Stephen Jn. *In the Crosshairs: Famous Assassinations
& Attempts From Julius Caesar to John Lennon*. Darby, PA:
Diane Publishing Co., 2003.

Time-Life Books. *Assassination*. New York: Time Life Education, 2004.

"Testimony of Mrs. John F. Kennedy." *The Warren Commis-
sion Hearings*, Volume V. www.aarclibrary.org/publib/jfk/
wc/wcvols/wh5/html/WC_Vol5_0095b.htm (accessed
January 7, 2013).

Clarke, James W. *American Assassins*. Princeton: Princeton
University Press, 1982.

Duersten, Matthew C. "The Man in the Santa Claus
Suit," *LA Weekly*, September 12, 2001. www.laweekly.
com/2001-09-20/news/the-man-in-the-santa-claus-suit/
full/ (accessed January 18, 2013).

Federal Bureau of Investigation. "Samuel Byck Dossier."
www.slideshare.net/InvestigatingtheTerror/sam-by-
ck-dossier (accessed January 18, 2013).

Linskey, Annie. "Policeman remembers his defin-
ing moment." *The Baltimore Sun*, November 13,
2005. http://articles.baltimoresun.com/2005-11-13/
news/0511120472_1_troyer-hijacker-ferndale (accessed
January 18, 2013).

Woestendiek, John. "The resurrection of Samuel Byck. Why
an almost forgotten would-be assassin has found an
audience after 30 years." *The Baltimore Sun*, February 6,
2005. www.10-digital.com/design/online/indigo/press/
samuel_byck.html (accessed January 18, 2013).

Associated Press. "3 Slain in Baltimore Skyjack Shootout."
Pittsburgh Post-Gazette, February 23, 1974. http://
news.google.com/newspapers?id=zstRAAAAIBAJ&s-
jid=_GwDAAAAIBAJ&pg=2067,2903113&dq=balti-
more+skyjack&hl=en (accessed April 29, 2013).

Chapters 11 and 12

Archibold, Randal C. "One of Ford's Would-Be Assassins Is
Paroled." *New York Times*, January 1, 2008. www.nytimes.
com/2008/01/01/us/01moore.html?_r=0 (accessed January 14, 2013).

Associated Press. "Sara Jane Moore fails in prison escape attempt." *Boca Raton News*, February 6, 1979.
http://news.google.com/newspapers?nid=1291&-
dat=19790206&id=thVUAAAAIBAJ&s-
jid=N40DAAAAIBAJ&pg=5073,1021484 (accessed
January 14, 2013).

Biography.com. "Squeaky Fromme." www.biography.com/
people/squeaky-fromme-20902443 (accessed January 14,
2013).

Bravin, Jess. *Squeaky: The Life and Times of Lynette Alice
Fromme*. New York: St. Martin's Griffin, 1998.

Brown, Angela K. "Lynette 'Squeaky' Fromme, Manson
Family Member Who Tried To Kill President Ford,
Released From Prison." *The Huffington Post*, August 14,
2009. www.huffingtonpost.com/2009/08/14/lynette-
squeaky-fromme-ma_0_n_259749.html (accessed January 14, 2013).

Bugliosi, Vincent and Curt Gentry. *Helter Skelter: The True
Story of the Manson Murders*. New York: W. W. Norton
& Company, 2001.

Clarke, James W. *American Assassins*. Princeton: Princeton
University Press, 1982.

Duke, Lynn. "Caught in Fate's Trajectory, Along With Gerald Ford." *The Washington Post*, December 31, 2006. www.washingtonpost.com/wp-dyn/content/article/2006/12/30/AR2006123000160.html (accessed January 14, 2013).

Fusco, Jennifer and Rocco LaDuca. "Would-be Ford assassin 'Squeaky' Fromme moving to Marcy." *Utica Observer-Dispatch*, September 14, 2009. www.uticaod.com/news/x211355264/Would-be-Ford-assassin-moving-to-Marcy (accessed January 14, 2013).

Gray, Charles F., Jr. "A Tribute to Thomas Jamison MacBride." *CourtHistory.org*. http://courthistory.tripod.com/macbride.html (accessed January 14, 2013).

Knight Ridder/Tribune News. "'Squeaky' Fromme unrepentant, still devoted to Manson." *Fort Worth Star-Telegram*, September 26, 2005.

Morrison, Pat. "Two gay heroes thwart assassinations—what a difference 35 years make." Los Angeles Times, January 10, 2011. http://opinion.latimes.com/opinionla/2011/01/two-gay-heroes-thwart-assassinations-what-a-difference-35-years-make.html (accessed January 14, 2013).

Shilts, Randy. *The Mayor of Castro Street: The Life and Times of Harvey Milk*. New York: St. Martin's Griffin, 1988.

Spieler, Geri. *Taking Aim at the President: The Remarkable Story of the Woman Who Shot at Gerald Ford*. New York: Palgrave Macmillan, 2008.

Spignesi, Stephen J. *In the Crosshairs: Famous Assassinations & Attempts From Julius Caesar to John Lennon*. Darby, PA: Diane Publishing Co., 2003.

Vronsky, Peter. *Female Serial Killers: How and Why Women Become Monsters*. New York: Berkley Trade, 2007.

Chapter 13

Caplan, Lincoln. *The Insanity Defense and the Trial of John W. Hinckley Jr.* New York: Laurel, 1987.

Clarke, James W. *On Being Mad on Merely Angry.* Princeton: Princeton University Press, 1990.

CNN.com. "Court gives would-be assassin John Hinckley more freedom." June 17, 2009. www.cnn.com/2009/CRIME/06/17/john.hinckley/index.html (accessed January 21, 2012).

Davidson, Osha Gray. *Under Fire: The Nra and the Battle for Gun Control.* Iowa City: University of Iowa Press, 1998.

Delahanty v. Hinckley, 564 A.2d 758 (D.C.App. 1989). www.titleii.com/bardwell/delahanty_v_hinckley.txt. (accessed January 21, 2012)

Linder, Doug. *Famous American Trials: The John Hinckley Trial,1982.* Columbia, MO: University of Missouri Press, 2008. http://law2.umkc.edu/faculty/projects/ftrials/hinckley/hinckleytrial.html. (accessed January 21, 2012)

Silverleib, Alan. "The day that changed presidential security forever." *CNN.com*, March 30, 2011. www.cnn.com/2011/POLITICS/03/30/hinckley.presidential.protection/index.html (accessed January 21, 2012).

Taylor, Stuart, Jr. "Hinckley Hails 'Historical' Shooting to Win Love." *New York Times*, July 9, 1982. www.nytimes.com/1982/07/09/us/hinckley-hails-historical-shooting-to-win-love.html (accessed January 21, 2012).

Wilber, Del Quentin. *Rawhide Down: The Near Assassination of Ronald Reagan.* New York: Henry Holt and Co., 2011.

Chapter 14

Gormley, Ken. *The Death of American Virtue: Clinton vs. Starr*. New York: Crown, 2010.

Leonard, Tom. "Osama bin Laden came within minutes of killing Bill Clinton." *The Telegraph*, December 22, 2009. www.telegraph.co.uk/news/worldnews/asia/philippines/6867331/Osama-bin-Laden-came-within-minutes-of-killing-Bill-Clinton.html (accessed January 17, 2012).

Sanger, David E. "Clinton Surveys Manila Bay: What, No Corncob Pipe?" *New York Times*, November 25, 1996. www.nytimes.com/1996/11/25/world/clinton-surveys-manila-bay-what-no-corncob-pipe.html?src=pm (accessed January 17, 2012).

Chapter 15

Bonner, Jessie L. and Jessica Gresko. "Oscar Ramiro Ortega-Hernandez Thought He Was Jesus, Obama Was Antichrist." *The Huffington Post*, November 18, 2011. www.huffingtonpost.com/2011/11/18/oscar-ortega-hernandez-jesus_n_1101222.html (accessed January 12, 2012).

Castillo, Mariano and Greg Botelho. "In video, White House shooting suspect calls himself 'modern-day Jesus'." *CNN*, November 18, 2011. www.cnn.com/2011/11/18/us/white-house-shooting-profile/index.html (accessed January 12, 2012).

Duggan, Paul. "Oscar Ramiro Ortega-Hernandez charged with attempt to assassinate Obama." *The Washington Post*. November 17, 2011. www.washingtonpost.com/blogs/crime-scene/post/oscar-ramiro-ortega-hernandez-charged-with-attempt-to-assassinate-obama/2011/11/17/gIQAZC9BVN_blog.html (accessed January 12, 2012).

FBI.gov. "Oscar Ramiro Ortega-Hernandez Indicted for Attempting to Assassinate the President of the United States." January 17, 2012. www.fbi.gov/washingtondc/press-releases/2012/oscar-ramiro-ortega-hernandez-indicted-for-attempting-to-assassinate-the-president-of-the-united-states (accessed January 12, 2012).

Savage, Charlie. "In Gunshots, a Trail of Threats Is Reported." *New York Times*, November 17, 2011. www.nytimes.com/2011/11/18/us/attempted-assassination-charge-in-shooting-at-white-house.html?pagewanted=all (accessed January 12, 2012).

Yardley, Willam. "White House Shooting Suspect's Path to Extremism." *New York Times*, November 20, 2011. www.nytimes.com/2011/11/21/us/oscar-ortega-white-house-shooting-suspect-struggled-with-mental-illness.html?ref=oscarramiroortegahernandez&_r=0 (accessed January 12, 2012).